Mobilizing for Compassion

DATE DUE

DEMCO 38-297

*M*obilizing for
*C*ompassion

Moving People
into Ministry

Robert E. Logan and Larry Short

Fleming H. Revell
A Division of Baker Book House Co
Grand Rapids, Michigan 49516

Published by Fleming H. Revell
a division of Baker Book House Company
P.O. Box 6287, Grand Rapids, MI 49516-6287

Printed in the United States of America

Library of Congress Cataloging-in-Publication Data

Logan, Robert E.

    Mobilizing for compassion / Robert E. Logan and Larry Short.
      p. cm.
    Includes index.
    ISBN 0-8007-5506-5
    1. Church work. 2. Church and social problems. I. Short, Larry. II. Title.
BV4400.L64 1994
253—dc20   93-38029

*To John Hayes and Royce Dunn, individuals
who have shown us Christ's character
through compassionate ministry*

$\mathcal{C}$ontents

_A_cknowledgments

We owe much to the dozens of ministry leaders who bore patiently our many questions, sent literature, gave tours of their projects, and helped in a multitude of other ways. God's presence and character is more evident through the loving work that each of you is doing.

"There is nothing new under the sun," wrote Solomon, and that is certainly true of the ideas contained within this book. We have gleaned ideas from many individuals who possess the brilliance we covet, including Peter Drucker, Stephen Covey, Charles Colson, Ray Bakke, George Barna, Gregg Cunningham, and countless others whose ideas and experiences influenced our thinking and contributed to this material.

Larry: Thanks for many mercies are due to my colleagues in ministry, who released me from my regular duties in order to complete this project. In particular, I think of Cory and Janet Trenda of Alternate Avenues Crisis Pregnancy Ministry; and of my friends and advisors, Scott and Rita Nelson, Ron Mueller, Craig Richardson, Stan and Deborah Maher, Royce Dunn, Bill Newsom, and Earl and Judy DeVries, as well as my brother and sister-in-law, Don and Gina Short, who provided much encouragement and support.

Special thanks is due to those who helped us gather research, manage our time, sift our ideas, and evaluate our progress: to Sonja Erickson, who telephoned countless ministry leaders and helped gather research, in addition to transcribing interviews; to my wonderful Alabama parents, Merl and Marge Short, as well as my sister and brother-in-law, Kay and Tom Knorr, for entertaining my kids during my travels; to my in-laws, Fred and Dorothy French, for allowing me to use their cabin as a writer's paradise; and to my beloved wife, Darlene, and children, Nathan and Mandy, for journeying with me and for allowing our home to be turned into a research center.

Most of all, though, I am grateful to my former pastor and current colleague, Bob Logan, who lives what he teaches and believes, and represents to me all that can be accomplished through Holy Spirit-inspired synergy, that process whereby the whole of an endeavor and a relationship between two people can be greater than the sum of its parts; as well as to his wife, Janet, for whom true biblical meekness, service, and grace are a way of life and an inspiration to many.

Bob: Special recognition needs to be given to my associate, Steve Ogne. Over the past three years, we have labored together, producing practical resources for church planters. Steve's wisdom and partnership in ministry is invaluable to me. Because of the similarities between new church developers and those desiring to start compassion ministries, many of the tools we developed have been adapted and incorporated into the fabric of this book.

I'm also grateful to Sam Metcalf, president of Church Resource Ministries, who read the manuscript and gave a number of valuable suggestions. Joan Florio, my secretary, helped with numerous details that enabled the book to be finished in a timely manner. Ed and Lou Carey helped us develop the appendices and improved the discussion of recovery ministry.

Without Larry Short's energy and creativity, this book would not be possible. He labored countless hours in research, writing, and editing. I count it a privilege to team with him on this book.

Together, we hope and pray that the Lord will mobilize his church for more effective compassion ministries. May the Lord guide you into appropriate applications for the advancement of God's kingdom.

Foreword

The debate gets tiring, especially for those of us who live in the trenches of ministry.

On one side are those fervently committed to the task of world evangelism and wanting to see heaven populated with redeemed individuals. On the other side are those whose hearts break for hurting humanity where oozing emotional and physical sores are graphic reminders of the flawed condition of the human soul.

My suspicion is that in his divinity, Jesus never struggled with such compartmentalization. Demonstrating compassion and simultaneously seeking the conversion of the heart were irrevocably welded and intertwined in the mind and ministry of the Son of God.

On a very practical level, that's what this book is all about.

Bob Logan is one of America's foremost authorities on church planting and a colleague who is committed to living out equally the mercy, justice, and love of Christ that the gospel demands. This volume seeks to provide a banquet table of encouragement to those committed to a ministry of evangelism that is powerfully integrated with a compassionate lifestyle.

And it's not written in an academic or theological ivory tower. It reflects years of pastoral experience and service among missionaries. I've personally observed Bob Logan with Church Resource Ministries (CRM) staff who live and minister around the world—among the poor of American inner cities, the suffering peoples of the former Soviet Bloc, or the affluent in industrialized nations such as Germany and Australia. Larry Short also writes from a background of rich ministry experience where he has sought to flesh out a compassionate lifestyle in the trenches of everyday reality. This volume has the ring of authenticity.

As one of the new missionary sodalities of the past decade, we hope that teams of CRM missionaries who are in the U.S. and around the globe will inculcate this vision for the holistic advance of the kingdom and expansion of the church. And what we seek in a missions setting is equally compelling for any local congregation of Christians, regardless of doctrinal uniqueness or polity distinctive.

It is high time that Christians regain their rightful role in society as people committed to the Great Commission and as people who live out the Great Commandment. I believe that when both are simultaneously operative, there will be greater hope for the sustained spiritual renewal in our generation for which we yearn.

May this book be a blessing and a challenge to the church as she strives to win people, not only to the Redeemer and Lover of their souls, but also to the One who is the Great Physician.

—Sam Metcalf
President, Church Resource Ministries

Introduction

The year was 30 A.D. The world was full of hurting people. Who was reaching out to them? Who was binding up their wounds? Who was bringing hope? And who was pointing a way to God? Only one person—Jesus of Nazareth—and his small band of followers.

Nearly two thousand years later, the world is still full of hurting people. Who is reaching out to them now? Who is binding up their wounds, bringing them hope, and pointing a way to God? Is it the government? The educational system? The business world? Or some other social institution?

Only one group is still motivated by unconditional love, exercising divine compassion, and pointing the way to God—*the body of Christ.* There is still only one person who can bring hope to the earth, only one Savior whose life and death is sufficient to redeem the entire world, and only one group of people to whom he has committed the task of compassion and the ministry of reconciliation—the church universal, the body of Christ.

Every day, more and more ordinary Christians are discovering the interdependent relationship between compassionate need-meeting ministry of all sorts and evangelism. Every day more and more ordinary Christians are beginning to reach out to their communities, self-sacrificially ministering through their own hurts and woundedness or through their prophetic calling to meet people's needs and point them to Christ. Every day more and more ordinary Christians give this vision for ministry a place in their hearts, and experience the breaking of God, which results in heartfelt compassion and mobilization to meet needs.

For Committed Christians Only!

This book is a *how-to manual* for those Christians who desire to find their place in ministry. It was a team effort by dozens of Christian ministry leaders from across the nation, people on the front lines who understand the need for practical tools to guide them in the establishment of effective, need-meeting ministries. It is not meant just to stir us up to go out and begin serving others; rather, it gives *practical assistance* in such nitty-gritty ministry areas as:

- How to truly listen to people and come to understand their needs
- How to listen to the Lord for a divine plan on how to creatively and effectively meet those needs
- How to recruit, motivate, train, and mobilize a team of people who will help you launch and operate your ministry
- How to develop a strategic plan for ministry
- How to launch a resource-efficient pilot project to test your ministry plans
- How to equip your ministry leaders for maximum effectiveness
- How to recognize and respond to various types of obstacles, deal with discouragement, and prevent burnout

A Vision for Ministry in the Last Days

Vision is a creative, two-part mental exercise in which we:

1. Come to perceive clearly the way things really are (objective reality)
2. Come to perceive clearly the way things ought to be, the way we believe God desires them to be (potential reality)

Many Christians believe that we are living in the last days, nearing the culmination of human history. What does the Bible say about the characteristics of the last days?

First of all, you must understand that in the last days scoffers will come, scoffing and following their own evil desires.

2 Peter 3:3

> But mark this: There will be terrible times in the last days. People will be lovers of themselves, lovers of money, boastful, proud, abusive, disobedient to their parents, ungrateful, unholy, without love, unforgiving, slanderous, without self-control, brutal, not lovers of the good, treacherous, rash, conceited, lovers of pleasure rather than lovers of God—having a form of godliness but denying its power.
>
> *2 Timothy 3:1–5*

Doesn't sound like ideal social conditions, does it? However, there is encouragement for the church in two other passages.

> "In the last days," God says, "I will pour out my Spirit on all people. Your sons and daughters will prophesy, your young men will see visions, your old men will dream dreams."
>
> *Acts 2:17*

> In the last days the mountain of the LORD's temple will be . . . above the hills, and peoples will stream to it.
>
> *Micah 4:1*

These dramatic events certainly do not predict a future without confrontation or suffering for Christians. No doubt casualties will mount as the battle between good and evil grows more intense. God's power will be manifested worldwide, and Christians will bear witness in the context of persecution and suffering. As the curtain finally closes on human history, the battle lines will become much more clearly drawn than they are now.

Rather than withdraw from the coming turmoil that awaits us at the end of human history—as too many Christians have done these last two thousand years—God is calling his church to embrace with anticipation and faithfulness the exciting days that lie ahead. He is calling us to deny ourselves, to take up our cross, and to follow him head-on into the fury!

The Nature of the Kingdom

When Christ spoke about the impact of the church on society, he never painted pictures of a social utopia. To the contrary, he frequently indicated that conflict would be, in many cases, the result of his coming. "I am sending you out like sheep among wolves," he said (Matt. 10:16). He indicated that we would be hauled before the authorities, arrested, and flogged. Brother would betray brother to death. All men would hate us, and we would be persecuted. In another place he said, "Do not suppose that I have come to bring peace to the earth. I did not come to bring peace, but a sword" (Matt. 10:34).

These were the events that would accompany the coming of the kingdom of God!

The kingdom of God is not easily defined. That is why Christ used a series of illustrations to teach it in a way the disciples could lay hold of it. That is why he asked the question, "What can the kingdom of God be likened to?" We must continue to ask that question in an attempt to get a handle on the rule of the kingdom of God in our lives, and to portray its import to others.

Christ painted a picture wherein people were governed by redeemed relationships, by godly values, by a common adoration of the role of the Holy Spirit within their hearts. We know now that the coming of this kingdom, at this stage of the game, is not simply an "event," but a "process." As we yield our hearts and lives to pour out his ministry through us, the kingdom of God will strengthen its grip on our hearts and will make its pervasive, holy influence known on our unholy world to an ever greater degree.

Think through your own vision.

If we are to see the kingdom of God expressed more and more in our midst, if we are to experience his unconditional love flowing through us, we must learn to *value people*. To value people is

- to come to *know* them, through incarnation (being with them where they are) and listening (two-way communication to come to understand *who* they are), and
- to *act* in order to meet their needs. "A man with leprosy came to [Christ] and begged him on his knees—'If you are willing, you can make me clean.' Filled with compassion, Jesus reached out his hand and touched the man. 'I am willing,' he said. 'Be clean!'" (Mark 1:40–41) Each of the seven times Scripture records that Jesus "had compassion," that compassion was immediately followed by *action* to meet human needs.

Valued people will become redeemed people when we have earned their trust and persuaded them, through both our words and our deeds, that the gospel really is the "Good News" that it claims to be;

that it is relevant to their lives. Redeemed people will then become discipled people as they commit their hearts daily to the Lord, become actively assimilated into the life of a healthy local church, and begin to use their gifts in interdependent ministry to others.

The Scope of Christian Compassion

Compassionate ministry is nothing new. Throughout history, God's people reached out in compassion to their neighbors in need. In the Old Testament, God instructed the Israelites to always leave the edges of their fields unharvested, to only harvest once, and to leave the crops unharvested one year out of seven—all in order to provide for the needs of the less fortunate among them, who were to be allowed to "glean" the fields without harassment.[1] The early church went a long step further, and reallocated resources to the needy and distributed food to widows.[2]

That famous English pastor, Charles H. Spurgeon, was not only one of the most popular preachers of all time, but he was also known for the need-meeting outreach ministries that seemed to pop up, like flowers sprung up in the meadow where Aslan danced, wherever this man of God cast his compassionate gaze. London was at that time, in the 1860s, the largest city in Europe, and possibly in all the world. Among Spurgeon's compassion ministries were an orphanage for boys, an orphanage for girls, a training college and a night school for the poor, a colportage (door-to-door literature and bookselling) ministry, which also visited the sick and in essence served a pastoral role in the community, free almshouses to shelter widows, food and clothing ministries, construction and community development ministries, and poor-children's schools. Somehow Spurgeon even found time to crusade against slavery![3]

Charles Colson notes that

in the nineteenth century, the church organized itself and went to the arenas of need: believers fed the hungry, clothed the poor, and housed the homeless. . . . [They] spearheaded most of our nation's significant works of mercy and moral betterment. They founded hospitals, colleges, and schools; they organized welfare assistance and fed the hungry; they campaigned to end abuses ranging from dueling to slavery. Though much of this work has now been taken over by government agencies, Christians provided the original impetus. . . . It was part of a rich evangelical tradition—and it put into practice the truth that in serving the least of Christ's brethren, we serve him.[4]

Today, Christians still contribute the bulk of resources for private charities of compassion.[5]

These examples of Christian compassion throughout history serve to challenge us to lift ourselves from the isolationism and self-serving mentality that has plagued the twentieth-century church. The good news is that today, compassion is being expressed more than ever before—and the potential is far greater still.

Many believers are beginning to turn to community outreach because they realize that there may be more to Christ-like service than simply singing in the choir on Sundays or organizing potlucks in the church fellowship hall. Christians who are burned-out after years of make-work ministry inside the church are discovering a new joy and a new sense of calling in offering that glass of cold water, in Jesus' name, to people in their community who are truly thirsty.

As you read this, in thousands of cities across the United States and throughout the world, Christians are conducting tens of thousands of unique and creative ministries. One outstanding example can be found in Chicago's inner city.

Lawndale Community Church is one urban church that is deeply committed to meeting the needs of its community and provides a model for other churches of exactly what can be accomplished.

"We seek to bring Christian holistic revitalization to the lives and environment of the residents of the *Lawndale Community*," reads their statement of mission, "through economic empowerment, housing improvement, educational enrichment, quality affordable health care, and Christian discipleship."

Few churches address issues like health care or housing in their statement of mission, but Lawndale does and focuses its energies accordingly. The entire church was named as one of President George Bush's "thousand points of light" in 1990. Springing from a church body of fifteen people in 1978, their worshipping congregation now numbers five hundred. But even this number belies the scope of their ministry in the community.

Lawndale's health clinic, considered one of the best medical clinics in America caring for the poor, was begun in 1984. Sixty staff members, including fourteen doctors, work to meet the health care needs of more than forty thousand people in the community. Nearly as many individuals work on staff with the church in other ways to meet other needs of the community. Much of the church's work in this regard is conducted through the Lawndale Christian Development Corporation of Chicago. They provide housing assistance, food, benevolence, and a gym ministry as just some of their outreaches.

The church's leaders recognize the importance of education, working redemptively within the Chicago public school system, through programs such as Project LEAP (one-on-one tutoring), computer classes, SAT and ACT preparation classes, and other basic-skills classes. Their college ministry seeks to assist people to enter college and build a support system enabling them to succeed and graduate, with the goal of raising up a new generation of black Christian leadership for the community.

Half a world away, evangelicals in Peru, according to a recent issue of *Christianity Today,* are converting their church buildings into soup kitchens, preparing meals for hungry families. Churches in the area are known for their efforts in tutoring and caring for orphans and other needy children as well as for fighting human-rights violations. The phenomenon coincides with the explosive growth of evangelical churches in Latin America.

There are churches in America, too, that have begun opening the doors of their buildings to the hungry in their communities. One such effort was begun by a married couples Sunday school class at The Church on the Way in Van Nuys, California. The idea got its start during a regular weekly potluck social. One of the couples, Dan and Jan Ross, said, "Here we are, having a good time and eating all this great food, while outside there are homeless and hungry people whom we sometimes step over on our way to worship. What are we going to do about it?"

The class took this couple's challenge seriously. They canvassed the area, got the word out through the Salvation Army, and opened the church's doors, inviting homeless people in off the street to be their guests at the potluck. Now, every Wednesday night the homeless eat at the tables while members of the church's worship teams bring music of peace, hope, worship, and life to the diners—just like at a fancy restaurant! Others sit and eat among their guests, getting to know who they are, where they are from, and what their needs are. The participants are invited to stay for a prayer meeting afterwards, where they not only continue to build a relationship with the believers, but also continue to build or establish their relationship with the Lord.

Today, in the Van Nuys area, no organization but the Salvation Army feeds more homeless people than that young marrieds Sunday school class!

Compassion: The Heart's Call to Action

We define *compassion*, as used in the title of this book, to be broader than a specific *function* like evangelism or social action. Compassion, as we use it in this book, does not simply refer to an emotion or a feeling either. When Christ had compassion it was a meeting of mind and heart that always resulted in the effective service of his fellow man. That service was not simply social action (as in feeding the five thousand) or evangelism (preaching to them of the coming kingdom of God), but a synthesis of both functions; they were interdependent and could not be separated one from another without diluting the effectiveness of the whole of Christ's compassionate ministry to us. Through acts of service he demonstrated that we desperately need him and he appealed to our hearts. Thus he prepared hearts to respond to the gospel that he taught through both word and deed. *Compassion* is therefore a mind *and* heart response of openness to God's leading, which arises from a personal observation of human need, physical and/or spiritual; and that leads to specific action taken to meet that need.

Mobilizing: Moving God's People Out

We define *mobilizing* as a two-step process that motivates believers for action and equips them for effective service. Mobilizing gets believers out of the pews and into the streets, where they can impact a hurting world for Christ.

This book, then, is a manual for motivating and equipping committed Christians not simply to experience an emotion, but to respond in obedience to God's leading, meeting physical and spiritual human needs.

America at a Crossroads

America stands at a crossroads today. The problems of poverty, urban violence, and human despair will not be addressed by government quick fixes. The kettles will continue to simmer and boil-overs like the 1992 Los Angeles riots will recur. Even as this book is being written, the radio blares news of new violence in the streets. Despair explodes into chaos when it sees its last hope taken away. Anarchy lies just around the corner—unless the church is revived spiritually and mobilized for action!

Ahead there is more pain, with no way to avoid it. We can undergo surgery or we can continue to suffer from the growth of our cancers. In both directions there are difficult days for America and the church. The church will survive both, but America may not. All nations eventually die.

Whichever road we choose (and at the moment it looks very much as if we may continue glibly down the broad path of destruction), the church must be ready to stand in the gap and meet the needs of hurting people. Our vision of a just and redeemed society is more desperately needed now than ever before. But more specifically, our compassion, our willingness to minister Christ's healing salve of mercy to the wounds of hurting people, is what America needs most at this juncture in her history. As Charles Colson says, "If we miss this opportunity, we will have little cause to quarrel with those who charge that Christianity is irrelevant."[6]

$\mathcal{1}$

$\mathcal{D}$eveloping a Vision for Compassion

Expand Your Horizons

What do the following people have in common?

- A baby is born with severe mental and physical disabilities. His parents are trying hard to cope, but all they can see ahead is a seemingly endless nightmare of doctor's appointments and medical bills. Their marriage is beginning to show the strains of long-term stress and fatigue. They would give anything for a weekend away! Meanwhile, the child's older, able-bodied sibling is starting to withdraw from school and exhibit antisocial behavior. His parents know the older child feels neglected, but they simply don't have the energy to deal with it.
- Two doors down, their neighbors are in the midst of a divorce. They have one daughter, age ten, who is convinced that she is to blame for the break-up. Knowing the custody battle that's ahead, both parents are maneuvering for her loyalty, and she feels pulled both ways. Each day as the little girl walks to school, she fantasizes about running away.
- Through the window of her tiny room in the local convalescent home, an elderly woman sits and watches the little girl walking along each morning. She fancies being a little girl again, with somewhere important to go and puddles to skip through and splash in. It's three months until Christmas, and she hopes the church people will come again to sing Christmas carols.

But otherwise, she receives no visitors, and sometimes she wonders whether she'll see another Christmas.

- The elderly woman envies her roommate, who has a thirty-four-year-old daughter who visits her every once in a while. The daughter is married and has two sweet children. She is visiting this morning and looks a bit haggard. Little do others suspect the reason. The woman is starting to have flashbacks about her dad's molesting her and has been getting almost no sleep.

- Six months earlier, the bed where the old woman now sits had been occupied by another, but she died. Her husband still attends the church around the corner; they gave him lots of support in the difficult days before the funeral, but since then no one has called. He recognizes what's happening, because he's done it himself many times—people are avoiding him because they don't know what to say and don't want to feel awkward. But the loneliness is killing him.

- Occasionally the man still gets a kindly call from his older sister. Her husband has Alzheimer's disease, and she watches in fear as her husband acts more and more irrational. The man knows that his sister, too, is beginning to slow down physically and to experience some health problems. What he doesn't know is how *trapped* she feels by the constant supervision that her husband requires.

- The couple has one daughter, but they haven't seen her in years. Although she is only forty-two, the woman is virtually confined to her home by chronic allergies to pesticides, perfume, detergents, and almost any other chemical or scent that can be transmitted through the air. Their family has been nearly destroyed by the high cost of medical care and the expensive water and air filtering systems installed in the house. The woman accepted the Lord one day after watching a Billy Graham crusade on TV, and would love to go to church, but knows that—with the Sunday morning crowd all freshly showered and perfumed and packed elbow to elbow in a confined space—church is the last place where someone with environmental illness can go.

- Across the street from this woman lives a teenager who contracted AIDS through a contaminated blood transfusion after a childhood accident. Even though she still seems quite healthy physically, the young woman cannot attend school because of the rejection, fear, and innuendo that her disease has caused.

- To complicate the family's problems further, the girl's father is a compulsive shopper and has been running up bills on the credit cards for years. His daughter's having AIDS hasn't stopped the spending. He is addicted to the newest technology and finds himself buying expensive items that he ends up never even taking out of the box. Collection agencies have been calling again, putting lots of additional stress on the marriage.
- Two doors to the south there is a twelve-year-old boy with a learning disability. Neil struggles constantly with a poor self-image. His dad left him and his mom when he was two, and his mother has to work long hours to make ends meet, so he spends most of his time alone, wandering the streets of his neighborhood. Yesterday he met a couple of boys in a club, who told him that if he passed an initiation (he doesn't understand the word but knows it would involve stealing a car), he could join their gang. He knows stealing is wrong but desperately wants to belong somewhere, and so he has decided that he will do it. Later that evening, after his mom leaves again, he dons a dark jacket and leaves the house.
- The gang's "headquarters" is in a shed behind an empty house, a block away. A family used to live in the house, but moved out after the husband lost his job as an engineer and they could no longer afford the rent. For the last month the family has been living in their old station wagon, parked in the shadows behind the neighborhood liquor store. As his family slumbers, the man reflects sadly, remembering how hard he once worked, and the many late hours that took him away from his family. Somehow he never seemed to be able to say no. Now the factory is gone, sold to another contractor and moved out of state. He was one of thousands "downsized" out of his job and, although he spends all day looking, he has found nothing even remotely close to his skills and abilities.
- Chatting with the clerk in the liquor store is a man with a similar plight, a man in a wheelchair. He was a successful business sales executive, forty-five years old, climbing the corporate ladder, when three years ago he suffered a near-fatal automobile accident. His lower back was severely injured and he lost the use of both legs. After a lengthy rehabilitation, he discovered that he no longer had a job to go back to. There was a time in his life when this man would have liked to have gone

to church. In fact, he tried it once but he decided it wasn't for him after he saw one of the deacons looking in dismay at a black skid mark the tire of his wheelchair had made on the white marble floor of the lobby. The restrooms there weren't wide enough for him anyway.

- As the man wheels out of the liquor store, he is propositioned by a surly looking youth. Clutching tightly the paper bag in his lap, he dismisses the sixteen-year-old boy with a wave of his hand, thinking, *Another punk!* The runaway teen meanders off, having learned by this time to stuff the feelings of rejection deep inside. Although he *had* been tempted to knock the man out of his chair, grab his bottle, and run, his memories of his last night in jail were still too fresh in his mind. So he continues wandering the streets. A lustrous black Cadillac pulls alongside, and its driver curses him—"You'd better get some work if you want to eat!" "Yeah, yeah, I'm tryin'," he says under his breath. He doesn't give the pimp the smart-mouthed answer he is thinking of, because he knows the man would just as soon kill him as look at him. *Just like my dad,* he thinks. When things get really bad he starts to think about going home, where at least there was good food on the table every night and he didn't have to endure the sweaty groping of disgusting old perverts in order to get it. But then he thinks about his dad and decides he would rather get kicked around by the pimp than have to go through again what his old man used to do to him. He steels himself, checks his swagger, and approaches another prospective customer, a man huddled anonymously in a large overcoat, plinking quarters into a sidewalk porno stand.

- The man seems very embarrassed to be approached by someone, and turns quickly away, stuffing his magazine into his coat pocket. *Another up-tight religious type,* the young man thinks before he turns away and goes to seek another "customer." The boy is closer to the mark than he realizes—the man, a leader in a local Christian church, struggles with a secret addiction to pornography. He wants desperately to get help, but doesn't know who he can trust with his terrible secret.

- As the church member retreats, he passes an olive-skinned man in tattered clothing, standing on the corner in the rain. The twenty-two-year-old man is an immigrant, who fled El Sal-

vador recently after his brother was killed by right-wing death
squads. He paid his entire life's savings to someone who would
smuggle him across Mexico and into California. Now he desperately needs a job, but doesn't know any English and hasn't
the faintest idea where to turn for help. Knowing he is an easy
mark for the sinister-looking gang of youths approaching him
from across the street, he hurries away in search of shelter.

Many Christians aren't involved in compassion ministries because
they don't see the need. That's rather like a fish complaining that he
can't see the water because it's not murky enough. The reality is,
wherever there are human beings, there are human hurts. If we are
surrounded with people, if we have our eyes open to our community
as we live our daily lives in it, we will see the ministry opportunities
that are all around us.

God doesn't ask us to meet all these needs all the time. But he
does ask us to meet the needs that we come across, one at a time. He
does ask us to offer a cup of cold water in Jesus' name.

Touching Today's Lepers

Geni Crupi is a registered nurse in Southern California whose first
job assignment was on an AIDS unit.

"At first it was very difficult. I walked in thinking, *Oh God, you
know this is the last place I want to be.*" But as Geni began working
with the terminally ill AIDS and HIV-positive patients, God began
to do a funny thing in her heart.

"For the first time, I began to see the inside person, the true victims of homosexuality and AIDS. God was saying to me very clearly,
You say you love people, so love some of these, society's most rejected.
I realized then that they are today's *lepers.* And what was Christ's
response to lepers? He courageously and compassionately reached
out and touched them."

At first Geni's approach toward the homosexuals was cautious. "I
was quiet, in a listening mode. But the men began to respond to me.
Not to my skills or my great learning, but they began to respond to
me in a way that I knew meant they were opening up and receiving
healing from the Lord. They responded to caring."

Homosexuals, Geni explains, have received so much condemnation from Christians that that is what they have come to expect. As a result they are thoroughly disarmed by nonjudgmental caring. "They know what they are doing is wrong," she explains, "better than anyone else. The Holy Spirit is the convicter of sin. But what are we as Christians called to do? As the church, we are a people who are called to accept and to reconcile people to God."

Geni realized the Lord was doing something unique in her life and ministry, but she still didn't know what form that would take.

In 1990 Geni's church, The Church on the Way, set up The Ministry Connection to showcase opportunities for ministry to the needy. Geni was invited to speak to the assembly about her experiences on the AIDS unit. "At this time," she says, "I didn't see myself as a leader. I was a resource person, someone who was available to whoever else wanted to start this ministry." But about seventy-five people turned out to attend her sessions, and thirty of those expressed an interest in being involved in ministry to AIDS sufferers.

"It all escalated from there. Out of those original thirty a very healthy core group of a half dozen people began to minister on a regular basis. Suddenly, I found myself leading this fledgling ministry, which we called Circle of Friends."

Geni's energy and enthusiasm for her ministry are contagious. "I'm pro-active in recruiting people," she explains. "Even if people are there just to observe or to get educated, I challenge them to become involved. I listen to the Lord while I'm talking to each person, and I ask him or her, *Why did you bring this person to me? What does he or she have to contribute to this ministry?*"

A foundation stone of the ministry is prayer. The group meets together each Saturday morning to seek the Lord's will. They seek practical opportunities to show compassion, moving out from that prayer foundation. "We might deliver a meal to an AIDS sufferer, or mow his lawn for him. We listen to them and try to discern their needs, then quietly do what we can to help." Geni finds that her volunteers are delighted to discover simple things they can do to truly minister to people in need.

Ministry Opportunities Abound

Reaching out to people with the AIDS virus is just one of hundreds of opportunities for believers to demonstrate godly compassion.

Steve Sjogren, pastor of Vineyard Christian Fellowship in Cincinnati, says the first step is to begin to ask the Lord to show you the pain of your community. "Ask the Lord for the gift of knowing and identifying your community's pain. Every city is unique in its problems, hurts, and pain."

Steve reminds us that few unchurched people are looking for a church. What they are looking for is a relief from their pain. If we can come to understand what that pain is, think creatively about ways to relieve it, and then demonstrate unconditional love, we will have come a long way toward the goal of reconciling those people to God.

Take a moment now to see how many different needs you can identify. Then compare your list to the one we compiled in appendix A. You may have identified needs that we didn't list; our list is certainly not comprehensive.

Research the Need

The age of information provides us with unique methods for coming to understand the needs of our communities, methods that have in few other cultures been available to the person on the street.

In order to avail yourself of these opportunities, there is one person in your community that you should get to know—the reference librarian at your local public library. Pastor Hal Seed, who is planting New Song Church in the Southern California community of Oceanside, tells about his experience.

"I walked up to the reference librarian and said, 'I need help in understanding who the people of this community are.' Without hesitation, she began pulling out the available resources—Bureau of the Census reports and other very helpful demographic information."

The Power of Visualization

We must recognize that true compassion is a work of the Holy Spirit, and it is his job to do that work within the hearts of those who are exposed to human suffering. However, it is our job as Christian leaders and as pastors to help our churches pull their heads out of

Sources of Information

Government Sources

Superintendent of Documents
Government Printing Office
Washington, DC 20402

Publication Sales and Services
Statistics Canada
Ottawa, Ontario, K1A 0V7

Data User Services Division
Customer Services (Maps)
Bureau of the Census
Washington, DC 20233
(301) 763-4100

Commercial Sources

CompuServe
(remote data access service
for personal computer users)
(800) 848-8199

Census Access for Planning in the Church

Concordia College
7400 Augusta Street
River Forest, IL 60305
(708) 771-8300

Church Information and
Development Services
151 Kalmus, Ste. A104
Costa Mesa, CA 92626
(714) 957-1282

Other Sources

Reference librarians (public
  libraries as well as local college
  and state university libraries)
Regional, county, and
  municipal planning agencies
School administrative offices
Chambers of commerce
Public utilities
Newspapers and radio
  stations
Real estate firms
Hospitals
Counselors
Churches
Ministry organizations

---

the sand and expose them to the full extent of the human need that surrounds us.

In the early eighties, when a massive Ethiopian famine was brewing, the staff of World Vision, International, and other Christian relief agencies experienced a great deal of frustration because they knew that a disaster of immense proportions was in the making, that would result in literally millions of children starving to death, yet in spite of their best efforts to warn the American public, we remained largely ignorant of the dilemma. It wasn't until the media began beaming images of pitiful, starving children, with their sunken eyes and swollen bellies and hideous, sticklike arms and legs, into the living rooms of America that the hearts of the viewing public were broken and compassion began to spring up. There was a generous outpouring of help—but not until it was too late for countless innocent children.

Experience the Need

How often do we really understand the pain that others suffer? Instead, our human nature is to take ourselves out of harm's way. A simple exercise conducted by JAF Ministries (formerly Joni and Friends Ministry) can give you just a small taste of the pain experienced by people with disabilities. During a church banquet or other group meal, divide the people up into five groups.

- Blindfold one group.
- Tie the hands behind the second group's backs.
- Tell the third group they cannot speak.
- Provide earplugs for the fourth group so that they cannot hear.
- Provide wheelchairs for members of the fifth group and tell them they cannot get out of them except to go to the bathroom, and even then they must not use their legs for support.

Such an exercise creates a quick dose of empathy toward people with physical disabilities. Tell people to imagine that experience being extended, that there is no hope of ever escaping that condition. Tell them to imagine further what life must be like for those who are learning impaired or mentally disabled, who struggle with self-esteem and must daily put up with the various attitudes of the able-bodied toward their disability.

Create Greater Awareness

Getting a hands-on introduction to living with a disability is just one example of how you can cultivate greater understanding of people's needs. Perhaps you can think of some others.

One youth group in the Los Angeles area actually became "homeless" for a night—walking the streets of their community with nothing but a blanket, visiting shelters and food pantries. One teen commented, "It was the first time I ever realized those were *real people* out there."

Many missions organizations provide short-term opportunities for involvement that are designed to help open Christians' eyes to inter-cultural and cross-cultural needs. One group takes church members on a three-week excursion to some of South America's more notable "dump cities" for an eye-opening intercultural experience. Other organizations specialize in taking groups of young people into dis-aster-stricken areas of the world for special-relief-team efforts. Such groups frequently find themselves nailing on new roofs after a hur-ricane or distributing food and blankets to the homeless.

A short-term cross-cultural experience can be life changing. Wit-ness the words of Alethea, a teen at Community Baptist Church of Alta Loma, California, who reflected in her journal about a weekend spent among the Oaxacan Indians in Maneandero, Mexico:

> The first camp we went to was mud and sage everywhere, with nothing but shacks all crammed together. The Oaxacan Indians gathered around the van as we got out. The children sure did remember the church van!
>
> We met Isabel, who shared her home with us. It was a card-board box, six feet on a side, and only four feet high. She showed us her Bible, and after a while we managed to under-stand her story. She reads to people every Sunday after she goes to church. Her Bible was highlighted and had a pretty white lace cover. It looked like the jewel of her possessions. When she brought it out of her little home, it glowed—kinda like her faith.
>
> The second camp was about as dirty as the first. We found a mother with an eight-month-old baby who was sick. She didn't look right, real overweight and almost swollen. In their home was a single, large black pot hanging over a fire.
>
> June and I offered the woman and her baby a ride back to the mission to see Val (the nurse). But the mother was too embarrassed to go because she was so dirty. Her pride kept her back, so we let her be.
>
> We walked with another poor woman, who had just lost her husband, back to her house. The pain and loneliness she was feeling made us very sad. We noticed a large piece of wood with a large cross on the top, probably a part of his coffin.
>
> I felt sad for everyone I met that day, because I wanted to help them but I knew I could only give them a bag of food and hopefully make them smile.

I see my life and compare, and I think, how sad! But this is the only life they know, and even though these people have so little, it's amazing how they can live so fully.

That night we sang. I felt like everyone in all of Mexico could hear us. That day had opened our eyes and touched our hearts. We will never forget the Oaxacan Indians.

Ministry Ideas to Consider

Just to get your idea juices flowing, here are a number of existing ministries that we discovered during our research. This is by no means a comprehensive list, for there are as many opportunities for compassion as there are human needs, and cataloguing them all would be nearly impossible. Consider these ideas to be food for thought, but don't be afraid to come up with your own.

Adult Victims of Child Abuse—Support groups for adult victims of child abuse (physical, sexual, or emotional) are growing rapidly, particularly on college campuses.

AIDS Ministries or Hospices—HIV-positive and AIDS-afflicted persons are the "untouchables" of our twentieth-century society. These ministries serve by providing companionship and by meeting physical, emotional, and spiritual needs.

Alternate Schools—"Private" education, not for the upper-middle class of a church's congregation, but for the poor and disadvantaged (maximum income levels set as requirements for entrance).

Child Advocates—Christians who take advantage of an opportunity and volunteer their time and efforts as a child advocate. They represent the needs of hurting, abused, and abandoned children in the courts, in foster homes, and in other similar situations.

Coffee Houses—A place for young people in the community to find refuge and human companionship. They use donated food and drinks, and provide Christian musicians, games, and space for conversation.

Computer Literacy—Teaching underprivileged or impoverished urban youth basic computer literacy skills can be a wonderful way to give them an interest in learning and a hope for rising to a place of self-sufficiency in a complex world.

Crisis Hotlines—Can be specialized (suicide, drug abuse, runaways, crisis pregnancy, etc.), or generic. Hotlines operate twenty-four hours a day, directing calls into the homes of trained volunteers. Companion ministries may be added as needed (counseling services, pregnancy testing, support groups, etc.).

Disability Ministry—Christians must take the lead in providing compassionate support for individuals experiencing physical or mental disablement. In some cases this may mean working voluntarily to make sure your church is more physically accessible to people who move about in a wheelchair, or to those who are visually impaired. It might mean providing qualified interpreters for the hearing impaired, or playing an advocacy role for the mentally disabled. Or it might be as simple as providing respite care for families with disabled children or parents. For a plethora of good ideas on ministering to people with disabilities and their families, contact JAF Ministries at P.O. Box 3333, Agoura Hills, CA 91301.

Disaster Relief Ministries—We all know about the large disaster relief organizations like World Vision, International; Food For The Hungry; and World Relief. Involvement by churches in the opportunities they offer is always welcome. Local churches can have an even greater impact by being prepared to serve in the event of earthquakes, floods, tornados, hurricanes, etc.

Divorce Recovery Ministries—With one out of three marriages failing, divorce is one of the most common need-generating phenomena in our culture. Failed marriages generate huge deficits in self-esteem in addition to causing depression and loneliness. Divorce recovery groups offer a biblical perspective, substantive help, and real support.

Economic and Community Development Ministries—Some ministries have extended the basic idea of shelter to the provision of a strategic plan for community and economic development—from a Christian perspective! One that we interviewed provides a transitional-permanent housing program, mobilizing "landlords with a heart" in the Los Angeles area. Homeless families living on skid row are placed, through a discipling process, into permanent housing through this ministry.

Elderly Ministries—The elderly, comprising a quickly growing segment of our society with specific needs for compassion, present a real opportunity for many churches and ministries. Frequently churches are asked to provide actual worship services on the premises of convalescent homes or retirement communities. Other ministries focus on hospice care, the provision of hot meals, special recreation or outings, Bible studies, or caring visitation. Often the needs of the elderly can be met very simply, by helping them fix a car or repair a washing machine, by driving them to a doctor's appointment, by cooking a hot meal, and so forth.

Employment Ministries—With approximately 10 percent of the employable people in the U.S. currently unemployed, the unemployed are one of the largest segments of hurting people in our nation. Employment ministries offer hope, encouragement, and help.

Ethnic and Urban Ministries—Ray Bakke points out that representative communities from most of the world's people groups have come to live in the cities of America. This provides a broad palette of opportunities for churches willing to target specific ethnic populations, for establishing support ministries, or for planting churches. One large church in the Los Angeles area has ministries working with Arabs, Armenians, Assyrians, African-Americans, Filipinos, Iranians, Jews, Latins, and Muslims. Other churches, which reside in areas with high concentrations of Asians, offer outreaches to Japanese, Chinese, Korean, Vietnamese, Cambodian, and many other ethnic groups. Outreaches to various American Indian cultures are offered primarily in southwestern states such as Arizona and New Mexico. An increasing number of believers are relocating to urban areas where they minister Christ's love and seek to establish new congregations that obey the Great Commandment and fulfill the Great Commission.

Food Ministries—Many fine examples of church-led food pantries abound throughout the U.S. Pay a visit to one near you for more information. Most act as a conduit between donated food (from local restaurants and markets as well as food distributors) and the person on the street. Some ministries reverse the expectation and actually take the food to the people; one in New York uses a hot-lunch truck, driving to areas where the hungry hang out, offering hot meals and a chance to listen to a gospel presentation.

Foster Homes—There is an urgent need for safe, stable, and compassionate homes where children can be placed on a short- or long-term basis. Christian foster parents have a tremendous opportunity to show unconditional love and caring, and groups that network the needs to these families are important partners in making this contribution.

Grief Ministries—Those who have lost loved ones through death or abandonment need a special touch of grace and mercy in their lives, particularly if they are children. Every church should have some internal form of grief-support ministry; but God will call some people to broaden the effort and actually take the ministry out into the community.

Health or Medical and Dental Clinics—Clinics offering free or reduced-rate health care in impoverished urban settings have proven to be an outstanding outreach offered by many inner-city churches and ministries.

Housing Ministries—As opposed to shelter ministries, housing ministries provide for the shelter needs of individuals on a long-term basis through such methods as the rehabilitation of substandard housing for the poor and homeless. Habitat for Humanity is one national organization providing leadership in the area of housing rehabilitation.

International Student Outreaches—At many U.S. universities, the majority of students hail from lands other than the U.S. These students spend two, four, or more years studying at our schools; then many depart for their home countries where they will take positions of leadership in their societies. Reaching an international student with the gospel can be as effective as or more effective than sending a full-time missionary to the faraway country from whence he or she comes!

Mediation Ministry—This ministry is specifically designed to mediate or arbitrate legal disputes or interpersonal conflicts, particularly among Christian brothers and sisters.

Mothers of Preschoolers (MOPS)—MOPS helps meet the needs of women by providing friendship and helping young moms grow in confidence and in parenting skills as well as spiritually closer to God. Activities are also planned for children.

Need Networking Services—Love Inc. is a unique ministry dedicated to helping local churches evaluate needs in their community and establish a plan to meet them in cooperation with other churches and social service providers in their community. Love Inc. does not itself establish programs to meet needs, but helps churches organize their people to minister on a person-to-person basis. It also works collaboratively with local service providers to establish effective, holistic care for the poor living in their community. For more information contact Love Inc.'s headquarters in the World Vision, International, office at Monrovia, California: (818) 357-7979.

Night Ministry—Urban night ministries are designed to provide emergency shelter and meet other needs of people who roam nightly the streets in our large cities.

Park Outreaches—In many urban settings and among certain cultures, the park is a "community center" and presents an opportunity for fair-weather outreach to large groups of people.

Pro-Life Ministries—In addition to crisis-pregnancy centers, shelters, and sidewalk-counseling ministries, there is a wide variety of types of pro-life ministries that provide education, adoption services, direct action, post-abortion counseling and referral, and political activism.

Prison and Jail Ministries—Charles Colson's Prison Fellowship is perhaps the best known ministry. But jail ministry throughout the U.S. does not stop there. There are many opportunities for Christian volunteers in juvenile detention, chaplaincy, and probation work. Some prison ministries focus on specific target groups among the prison population, like women inmates or the families of inmates; others are involved in pen-pal ministries with inmates; still others focus on giving support to inmates once they are released.

Prostitution—Greenlight is an outreach ministry of the Ichthus Christian Fellowship in London, seeking to build redemptive relationships with a community of so-called professional prostitutes in London. Women from Greenlight visit fifty prostitutes on a regular basis, offering friendship and support.

Refugees—Refugees fleeing poor economic and political conditions pour into the U.S. by the thousands each day. Christians can minister to them by providing trained advocacy and counseling regarding their occupational, housing, and health concerns. Most refugees need basic training in English. Some refugee groups need sponsorship and assistance as they seek to immigrate.

Runaways—In most large cities there are literally thousands of runaway children living on the streets. They need food and shelter, health care, advocacy, and a Christian group to give them a sense of belonging.

Shelter Homes—Sheltering ministries come in many, many flavors. There are urban shelters, shelters for abused and battered women, and shelters for those in crisis pregnancies. Some offer help to women who are the victims of marriages destroyed by substance abuse, assisting them in providing for dependent children as well as meeting their own needs.

Substance Abuse—There is a place for alcohol and drug-abuse support groups in every church, as well as groups targeting such affected others as spouses and adult children of alcoholics. Another offshoot is support groups dealing with the issue of codependency, the phenomenon whereby negative habits are unwittingly supported by family members and loved ones.

Terminally Ill—Hospice-care ministries provide compassionate care to the chronically or terminally ill. Some specialize in a certain disease, like AIDS or HIV; others provide care for a segment of the population, like the elderly.

Vietnam Veterans Outreaches—Vietnam veterans constitute a large group of individuals in our society who have unique and often challenging needs. According to one outreach ministry, 40 percent will never admit publicly that they served in Vietnam! Yet few ministries and churches have been established to reach out specifically to these individuals. Marvelous opportunities are available to those who are willing to minister in this area.

Don't Be Overwhelmed

We live in a needy world, and when a person sits back and seeks to learn of those needs, it's easy to get overwhelmed. So many opportunities, so little time! In looking at your community you'll find yourself wishing you had many lifetimes to give to meeting the needs that you will discover. There is no lack of worthy causes—ministries that feed the hungry, visit prisoners, give shelter to the homeless, serve disabled people and their families, provide job training for urban youth—and each begs for our attention.

One day as Christ was speaking with his disciples in the open countryside, he directed their attention to a field, white with harvest, and said, "The harvest is plentiful but the workers are few. Ask the Lord of the harvest, therefore, to send out workers into his harvest field" (Matt. 9:37–38).

This takes a certain amount of pressure off our shoulders. He said, "Pray for workers" (plural!). He recognized the fact that it would be a big harvest, and it would be impossible for any one individual to meet every need. His plan is for us all to work *together.* But the important point is: We must all find our part and do it.

As a committed Christian, you have a big heart, and it's soft before the Lord. You want to help. And so you find yourself susceptible to everyone who comes along and tells you about a real need. Soon you are doing everything—and then you burn out, and you can't do anything.

No, we *can't* do everything. We hope that this book will free you from the tyranny of feeling that you have to exhibit a response to every one of the world's problems. The key question is, how do you focus in on the most important ministry for *your* life? How do you discover that passion? What are you skilled and gifted to do? What is that specific area of ministry to which God has called you? How do you hear his quiet voice?

The next step is to discern God's calling for your life—the unique contribution through which you can express compassion to a needy world.

Action Idea Checklist

☐ Ask the Lord to show you the pain in your community.

☐ Get on the mailing list of local and national compassion ministries to increase awareness and maintain contact.

☐ Discover needs and compassion-ministry opportunities in your community. Keep an updated list of compassion ministries for networking and referrals.

☐ Interview leaders doing compassion ministry; go and see their ministry in action when possible.

☐ Sponsor a ministry-awareness day at your church. As broadly as possible expose people to needs in the community. Highlight your church's compassion ministries and invite other effective agencies to participate.

☐ Write out your vision for compassion ministry in your church or organization.

Add your own follow-up items below.

2

*C*ultivating a Passion for Compassion

Hearing the Call

You've heard the story of Cinderella? You know, the one where the handsome prince searches the kingdom for his pretty young soul mate?

Well, the story of Esther is a biblical Cinderella story—with a twist.

Esther was a Jew during one of the many periods of history when it wasn't very popular to be one. This time, the Jews were in captivity in Persia. King Xerxes, the king of Persia and Media, had ousted his previous queen and had ordered a kingdomwide woman hunt for the most beautiful virgin in all of the kingdom who would become his new queen.

Esther fit the bill. She was so beautiful that those who found her were conveniently able to forget that she was Jewish when they presented her to the king.

Esther had an uncle, a God-fearing man named Mordecai, who had once done a service to the king by revealing a plot against his life, a service that was promptly forgotten in the course of things. One of the king's chief officials, however, an evil man named Haman, hated Jews in general and Mordecai in particular for his refusal to worship idols. Haman influenced the king to issue a genocidal edict against the Jews and had a gallows built on which he personally planned to hang Mordecai.

As things turned out, Queen Esther was the only one in a position to save the day. But doing so would entail no small risk to her own neck. Uncle Mordecai advised, "If you remain silent at this time, relief and deliverance for the Jews will arise from another place, but you and your father's family will perish. And who knows but that you have come to royal position for such a time as this?" (Esther 4:14).

This is a phenomenal thing to think about. What are you saying, Mordecai? Do you mean to tell us that Esther's selection as queen was specifically designed so that she might some day be in this position to intervene? That God endowed her with beauty, grace, intelligence, and all the other things that had caught King X's royal eye, simply for that purpose?

Fortunately for the Jews, Esther acknowledged God's special calling on her life: "If I perish, I perish." She recognized God's hand in her life and had a passion for God's people that motivated her to courageously act on their behalf.

God had raised up Esther to fulfill a very special niche. That's true with all of us. Ephesians 2:10 says, "For we are God's workmanship, created in Christ Jesus to do good works, which God prepared in advance for us to do."

God has created us as members of one body, but each of us has a different function, a unique role to play. Each of us has a unique mix of passion, gifting, personality, skills, and talents, which all work together to equip us perfectly either for that moment in time when God calls on us to play our crucial hand; or else, which is more likely, to that work of ministry, whether it be months, years, or decades in duration, where we can be most effectively used to help bring about the purposes of God.

What's Your Passion?

In the last chapter we defined *vision* as getting a clear and accurate understanding of both the way things are and the way they ought to be. Where vision deals largely with the mind, passion deals largely with the heart. By *heart*, we do not simply mean emotions; for emotions change from day to day and week to week. Passion is much broader than this; it is the deep motivational drive that shapes our vision.

As we interviewed ministry leaders across the nation in preparation for this book, we noticed an interesting phenomenon. Every single leader of an effective compassion ministry we spoke with was driven with an intense *passion* for that ministry. Why, they seemed to feel as if their specific area of need-meeting ministry was the most crucial on the planet! Those who ministered to the poor pointed out all the many Scriptures about how God sides with the poor. Those who ministered to the disabled pointed out how Christ spent so much time healing the disabled. Those who did pro-life ministry said, "Your compassion isn't really compassion unless you speak out on behalf of the most innocent of human beings, unborn children dying in the womb." Those who fed the hungry, clothed the naked, and visited prisoners pointed out Christ's watershed words about these activities in Matthew 25. Those whose passion was orphaned children or ministry to widows invoked the words of James 1:27 about "true religion."

Each leader we spoke with saw the value of all these different types of ministry and recognized logically the principle of diversity of ministry. But in their *hearts,* the most important needs were those that God had impassioned them personally to meet!

That's passion. By definition, it entails *imbalance.* It is a single-minded focus. It involves the meaning of your life, the purpose of your existence; all else pales by comparison. We believe this drive—so misunderstood by those who have not yet experienced it—has been placed by God in the human heart because he knows that's what it will take to get the job done.

A Matter of the Heart

Passion is God-given, and therefore should be discerned in prayer. As a part of this prayerful process, it helps to look at giftedness, personality, learned skills, talents, and heart desire.

As an example, take John the Baptist. John shared the same basic vision of the one whose coming he announced—"the Kingdom of God is at hand." But John was amazingly *impassioned* by God to do a work of ministry that specifically involved preparing the way for the Christ—not only announcing his coming, but preaching repentance to the Israelites so that their hearts might be softened to the coming of the Messiah.

We would say that John was "cut out" for this role:

His gifts—Prophecy, preaching, discernment, he had a gift mix that uniquely qualified him for his ministry.

His skills—John spent his life in the wilderness, in meditation and worship, getting to know personally the God whose advent he would proclaim. He also developed significant leadership skills; his band of followers was fiercely loyal. Moreover he developed some very unique wilderness skills, which few others would appreciate, like wearing scratchy skins of wild beasts, eating bugs, and rooting out wild honey (which no doubt meant coping with angry bees!).

His personality—John was intensely focused on his goal, preparing the way for the Messiah—so focused that he was probably the only person in history who began actively fulfilling his job assignment before he was even born! The way in which he interacted with others perfectly suited his role as the announcer of the Messiah. He was tough, bold, and challenging to the point of being abrasive.

His character—John was humble; he had to be, for he knew from the day of his birth that he was the announcer and not the main attraction. He was willing to step aside once the Messiah had been baptized. He was no respecter of persons and pulled no punches even with Herod the king. He didn't care what others thought of him, never hesitated to tell the truth, and only once did he express any reservations about his mission. He was fearless and went to his death without flinching. Christ honored him as the greatest prophet of his day.

John was anointed from before his birth to perform the role that God had impassioned him to perform. His life was a very clear case of divine intervention!

Will others be able to look at our lives and say the same thing? Are we cut out for a specific God-given purpose? Will they say about us, "That's what he or she was created to do or be?"

Just as the heart is central to the body, your passion is central to your being. Historically, we look at certain individuals and realize they had a passion for what they were and did, whether for good or for ill. Napoleon had a passion for conquering. Mother Teresa has a passion for giving comfort to the afflicted. Mr. Rogers has a passion for identifying with and introducing children to the world at large. Margaret Sanger had a passion for population control. Hitler had a passion for eugenics. Ben Franklin had a passion for invention. Mozart had a passion for music. Martin Luther King, Jr., had a passion for racial justice. The list goes on and on. When we mention these individuals' names, we think readily of their passion, because it is the identifying characteristic of their being.

You can do a job because it's a duty, and you might even do it well, but you cannot do it outstandingly if it is not a passion of your heart. Passion alone provides motivation for vision and turns dreams into reality.

How Do You Get Passion?

We have identified three principle ways that passion comes to people:

1. Through our personal woundedness
2. Through our life situation
3. By divine call

Passion Through Personal Woundedness

The Age of Rage

Observers have coined the age in which we live, The Age of Rage. Eight out of ten Americans have been deeply wounded by either some sort of abuse, serious antisocial behavior, or uncontrolled addiction such as:

- Child abuse (physical, mental, or emotional)
- Sexual abuse
- Spousal abuse (physical, mental, or emotional)
- Rape
- Incest
- Abortion
- Violent crime
- Compulsive sexual behavior
- Compulsive eating disorders
- Alcoholism
- Drug abuse
- Family member of an alcoholic or drug abuser

Most of us have either suffered from one or more of these tragedies or have a close relationship with someone who has.

In recent years a great deal of excitement, and even some controversy, has swirled around the implications of the woundedness of Americans and their ministry in our churches. A thousand varieties of recovery groups and courses have sprung up to meet the needs of specific categories of wounded people. People have discovered relief from their pain in the sharing of it with small groups of other, similarly afflicted individuals, and in dealing with it in a manner that will eventually lead to healing, or at least to a process of healing.

One of the original and most popular programs for recovery groups is the Twelve Step program. The first Twelve Step program was begun by the organization Alcoholics Anonymous as a method of helping alcoholics to find healing, and it was secular in nature. What many people don't realize is that the principles governing each of the Twelve Steps themselves were taken from the pages of Scripture (see appendix B for a version of the Twelve Steps used by some Christian groups, accompanied by Scripture references for each step). Even though the Twelve Steps have biblical roots, the method has been the subject of some controversy, accused of being extra-biblical and insufficiently Christ-centered. Although it is not our intention here to provide an in-depth theology of the Twelve Steps, it has been our experience that this method and other similar methods have brought a great number of people freedom and healing from their hurts and addictions through the application of biblical truth to their lives. In addition, and most importantly, we have seen many people come to Christ through the Twelve Step program.

Some pastors may be uncomfortable with the fact that the demand for recovery is at least partly due to this cultural self-worship phenomenon of recent years—the fixation on personal health and wholeness. But beyond this discomfort, few could deny that the recovery movement presents a marvelous opportunity for compassionate outreach ministry to hurting people in our communities, people whose real and most deep-seated need is for Christ to fill the God-shaped vacuum within their souls; but who may experience and express this need in different ways, primarily as a need for wholeness and recovery from some addiction or for peace about some injurious event of their past.

Frequently, when pastors and lay leaders look at their communities and ask themselves, exactly what is it these people need? what is it that will push their buttons? They are looking for different types of answers. They are looking for answers like: We need fellowship, friendship, or, We need some place where our kids can learn how to share as well as learn why they should stop hitting each other, or, We need to cut loose in a place that really knows how to sing those jazzy choruses. They aren't looking for answers like: I need to know how to stop drinking and put my family and my life back together, or, I need to understand how my feelings of worthlessness and my present relationships with my kids are affected by the fact that my dad used to beat me until my legs bled, or, I need to figure out how to stop feeling so ashamed and guilty about the abortions I had when I was a teenager, and the needs that I had that drove me to ignore precautions and become pregnant repeatedly.

It is our natural tendency as people, as churches, and as Christian leaders, to ignore hurting segments of our society. No one *likes* to be around pain. So we, subconsciously perhaps, isolate ourselves from it, build our churches in such a way that we won't have to deal with it.

But in so doing we miss out on many of the opportunities that God is bringing to our doorstep. As the old adage goes, "Behind every cloud there is a silver lining." If you dodge the clouds, you miss the silver linings as well.

Peter Drucker notes that one of the characteristics of successful innovators is their capacity to see the glass half-full rather than half-empty.

Larry Short relates that this is one of the qualities demonstrated by his six-year-old daughter, Amanda.

This morning, our dog—a sturdy mutt of indeterminate genetic lineage—was pulling us to school as usual. Mandy had hold of the leash with one hand and was dragging me along behind with the other. As we walked we were discussing the relative merits of having two legs versus having four. Mandy, as usual, was seeing the best sides of both situations.

"They can sure pull a lot harder with four legs than we can with two," I noted breathlessly, starting the ball rolling.

"But they don't have any arms," she said observantly. "We hug a lot better."

"That's true," I admitted. "But if they get a thorn in one paw, they can still go along better on three legs than we can hop on one if we hurt one foot."

Then Mandy thought a bit before she came up with the clincher. "Yes," she glowed, "but we fall down better!" For Mandy—as everyone in our neighborhood knows—falling down is a fine art.

Americans have become adept at the art of falling down and hurting themselves. We can perceive this fact as a glass half-empty: "If only our church weren't so full of dysfunctional people, then maybe we could *do something* for the Lord!" Or we can perceive it as a glass half-full: "So, eight-out-of-ten people in our church are wounded. Think of all the opportunities for ministry! Think of what will happen in this church if we are successful in beginning to help these individuals on to a road of healing from their pain! Think of all the people in the neighborhood who will hear of it and who will want to come and be a part!"

A Biblical Perspective of Woundedness

No individual is better able to give empathetic, motivated assistance to a person in need than a person who has experienced that need for himself or herself, and who understands the road to freedom as a result of his or her own healing experience.

This is the central fact of Christ's own ministry to us. We were unredeemed until "he who knew no sin became sin on our behalf."

> He was despised and rejected by men, a man of sorrows, and familiar with suffering. Like one from whom men hide their faces he was despised, and we esteemed him not.
> Surely he took up our infirmities and carried our sorrows, yet we considered him stricken by God, smitten by him, and afflicted.
> But he was pierced for our transgressions, he was crushed for our iniquities; the punishment that brought us peace was upon him, and by his wounds we are healed.
> We all, like sheep, have gone astray, each of us has turned to his own way; and the LORD has laid on him the iniquity of us all.
>
> *Isaiah 53:3–6*

In Philippians 2:6–8, Paul says that Jesus,

> being in very nature God, did not consider equality with God something to be grasped, but made himself nothing, taking the very nature of a servant, being made in human likeness. And being found in appearance as a man, he humbled himself and became obedient to death—even death on a cross!

The author of the letter to the Hebrews wrote, "For we do not have a high priest who is unable to sympathize with our weaknesses, but we have one who has been tempted in every way, just as we are—yet was without sin" (4:15).

Our fundamental woundedness, as human beings, is the common experience of our susceptibility to sin and temptation. Our struggle with our sin natures and our sin habits is the greatest struggle, the greatest handicap, that any of us faces in life. Clearly this is a handicap not shared by the Creator of the cosmos. But can he *sympathize* with our struggle? Yes! His compassion is empathetic, because of the fact stated in Hebrews 4:15—he became flesh and was tempted just as we are—and yet without sin. *He knows what it feels like to be tempted.* This knowledge, this observation, leads him into profound compassion for our condition; and his compassion always leads to action on our behalf. His greatest sacrificial act, his substitutionary death on the cross, arose out of his compassion for us and is the one and only thing in this entire universe that can bring us healing from the woundedness of sin!

The Chronicles of the Wounded

The Bible is full of stories of the wounded. Some of them make entirely unlikely heroes. Rahab was a prostitute in Jericho, but because she saw what the Lord was doing and was willing to submit to it, she became a biblical example of faith and the forebearer of the Messiah himself. Mary Magdalene was a disciple of Jesus' who had been delivered of seven demons (Mark 16:9). She was a dear friend and follower of the Lord, the last to leave his side at the cross, and the first to discover the empty tomb. She was also the very first person to whom he appeared following his resurrection. It is thought that she may be the unidentified harlot of Luke 7:37–38 who expressed her gratitude and worship for being freed from her life of pain by anointing Christ's feet with perfume and tears, then wiping them with her hair. No doubt as she followed the Lord she was able to have an impact on the many women who sought deliverance from lifestyles of oppression.

Another story in the Bible demonstrates how highly God values the ministry efforts of the wounded. The demoniac of the Gerasenes was a man who had experienced pain on a level that few of us could ever comprehend. This man lived in the cemetery—right in the tombs with the dead bodies. In his madness, he ran around naked, cutting himself with stones and crying out night and day. For such a man there was no sleep, no rest.

> When he saw Jesus from a distance, he ran and fell on his knees in front of him. He shouted at the top of his voice, "What do you want with me, Jesus, Son of the Most High God? Swear to God that you won't torture me!" For Jesus had said to him, "Come out of this man, you evil spirit!"
> Then Jesus asked him, "What is your name?"
> "My name is Legion," he replied, "for we are many." And he begged Jesus again and again not to send them out of the area.
>
> *Mark 5:6–10*

The demons requested that they be sent instead into a nearby group of pigs, and Christ complied. The pigs then hurled themselves down the hill and drowned in the sea. The owners of the pigs rushed into town to tell everyone there what had happened (doubtless they were rounding up a posse of sufficient size to where they felt they would be able to dictate terms to Jesus and his disciples).

> When they came to Jesus, they saw the man who had been possessed by the legion of demons, sitting there, dressed and in his right mind; and they were afraid. Those who had seen it told the people what had happened to the demon-possessed man—and told about the pigs as well. Then the people began to plead with Jesus to leave their region.
> As Jesus was getting into the boat, the man who had been demon-possessed begged to go with him. Jesus did not let him, but said, "Go home to your family and tell them how much the Lord has done for you, and how he has had mercy on you." So the man went away and began to tell in the Decapolis how much Jesus had done for him. And all the people were amazed.
>
> *Mark 5:15–20*

This story demonstrates how valuable wounded people are to God. Why would Jesus turn down this man's request to follow him? After all, he had actively recruited literally hundreds of followers. Besides, it was Christ who said, "whoever comes to me I will never drive away" (John 6:37). But Christ knew the power of the witness of this man's healing. Doubtless there were others similarly oppressed in his area. In what appears to be a parallel account of this event (Matt. 8:28–34), two demoniacs are involved. Christ instructed the man to simply go home and tell his family "how much the Lord has done for you, and how he has had mercy on you," but this particular wounded healer didn't stop with just his family; he traveled throughout the entire ten-city area known as the Decapolis telling his story, so that "all the people were amazed." Apparently this man had quite a reputation.

Yet another "wounded healer" in the Scriptures was the man Christ healed who had been born blind. The snippet of conversation between Christ and his disciples about this man reveals at least a partial answer to the question: Why do people suffer?

> His disciples asked him, "Rabbi, who sinned, this man or his parents, that he was born blind?"
>
> "Neither this man nor his parents sinned," said Jesus, "but this happened so that the work of God might be displayed in his life. As long as it is day, we must do the work of him who sent me. Night is coming, when no one can work. While I am in the world, I am the light of the world."
>
> *John 9:2–5*

The purpose for this particular man's suffering was so that *the work of God might be displayed in his life*. That work of God was the healing from blindness that followed (6–7), and the implications of this healing astonished the man's neighbors (8–12), stunning, shaming, and angering the Pharisees (13–34), condemning them with the knowledge of who Christ was. The final result of this work of healing was the moving story of the man's spiritual healing.

> Jesus heard that they had thrown him out, and when he found him, he said, "Do you believe in the Son of Man?"
>
> "Who is he, sir?" the man asked. "Tell me so that I may believe in him."
>
> Jesus said, "You have now seen him; in fact, he is the one speaking with you."
>
> Then the man said, "Lord, I believe," and he worshiped him.
>
> *John 9:35–38*

The implications of this story are staggering. Clearly, there are those whose affliction has been allowed expressly for the purpose of being healed, therefore bringing God glory. Such was the case with the man born blind.

But what if Christ had not taken it on himself to heal this man? What if this had been a missed opportunity? The man would have continued in his blindness—physically and spiritually. There would have been no witness to his neighbors, his parents, his friends; no calling of the Pharisees to accountability. The man would never have had the encounter with the living Christ. His story would have been unrecorded, robbing all of us of its benefit. His life of suffering would have been a tragic and colossal waste.

Ephesians 2:10 declares, "For we are God's workmanship, created in Christ Jesus to do good works, which God prepared in advance for us to do." God has prepared, in advance, opportunities for us to do good works that display his power and glory! Among these good works are acts of redeeming woundedness, acts of physical and spiritual healing. Our own woundedness may have been allowed to occur for this purpose. God allows this pain so that his power may be displayed—and he chooses to display his power through us! As Paul says in 2 Corinthians 1:3–4,

> Praise be to the God and Father of our Lord Jesus Christ, the Father of compassion and the God of all comfort, who comforts us in all our troubles, so that we can comfort those in any trouble with the comfort we ourselves have received from God.

Is it possible for us to refuse or neglect to "walk in" the good works that God has prepared for us to do? Apparently the answer is yes. We may, through our own ignorance, disobedience, or fear, miss the opportunities that God provides.

There is an intriguing relationship in the Gospels between physical and spiritual woundedness. Several times, we glimpse that the more *significant* act that Christ conducts is the act of spiritual healing. The healing of the paralytic gives another example of a man healed both physically and spiritually:

> Some men brought to him a paralytic, lying on a mat. When Jesus saw their faith, he said to the paralytic, "Take heart, son; your sins are forgiven."

At this, some of the teachers of the law said to themselves, "This fellow is blaspheming!"

Knowing their thoughts, Jesus said, "Why do you entertain evil thoughts in your hearts? Which is easier: to say, 'Your sins are forgiven,' or to say, 'Get up and walk'? But so that you may know that the Son of Man has authority on earth to forgive sins. . . ." Then he said to the paralytic, "Get up, take your mat and go home." And the man got up and went home. When the crowd saw this, they were filled with awe; and they praised God, who had given such authority to men.

Matthew 9:2–8

Christ gave us, by example and by command, the imperative and the authority to heal both physically and spiritually. We are not *just* to preach forgiveness of sins, and we are not *just* to offer a cup of cold water in his name. Both go hand in hand. Our task of reconciliation involves the *whole person*—physical, mental, and spiritual.

Understanding Our Woundedness

Each of us experiences need; it's part of being human. It is easy to look at a person like the Prodigal Son, and say, "Gee, that guy was really messed up, and look how much the Lord forgave him! Look what he saved that boy from!" But one doesn't look at someone like the Prodigal Son's older brother, the one who never strayed, the one who never experienced the full onslaught of the world's barbs, and think, *Now, there's a wounded person.*

Nonetheless, the truth is that the older brothers, the faithful sons, are also wounded. The authors of this book are both second-generation Christians, baby boomers born into families that loved Christ and professed his lordship. We both made confessions of faith at an early age rather than waiting until we were twentysomething and mired deeply in the ways of the world.

But that doesn't mean there are no dark areas of our life that need Christ's healing. Bob Logan, for example, had to deal with his own drivenness and perfectionism, having been raised in a high-achievement family. Larry Short confides that he struggles frequently with issues of pride, impatience, and a tongue that occasionally gets him into trouble. Just as the Prodigal Son's older brother had to deal with his own bitterness and self-centeredness, so too second- and third-generation Christians—those whom others might think "have it all together"—struggle with their own hurts and needs.

We need to identify our own areas of hurt, and realize that our ministry to others might flow out of these areas of woundedness. For instance, our woundedness may have given us a particularly acute understanding of the extent to which we need the Lord; thus we understand more easily the simple fact that people need the Lord, and we become his evangelists. For Bob, the pain of trying to plant a church with inadequate resources and coaching led him to dedicate his life to serving new church developers.

For some, that woundedness runs deeper. It may even be buried well below the surface of our everyday lives, perhaps even in our subconsciousness.

Mike's Story

Mike (not his real name) was fresh out of his second broken marriage when he came to the Lord about ten years ago. Mike was forty-five at the time. He was listening to a Christian radio station in his car during his lunch break when a preacher shared his testimony and challenged his listeners to give their lives to Christ. Mike says it was the first time since he was a kid that he broke down and wept.

Mike knew he brought much baggage, and many hurts, to this new relationship with his Creator. Two broken marriages, a son on drugs, a daughter who had wandered away to slip into a river and drown when she was two, and a substance addiction or two of his own—Mike's past life was a lot to be saved from, and he was grateful every day for the Lord's forgiveness and cleansing.

But after five years had gone by, Mike somehow knew that there was something more. Christian friends he had grown close to in the previous few years could sense it too, and they were praying for him. Then, one night, it all came to a head. At a church meeting, Mike listened to the emotional story of a man who had been abused as a child. Afterward, choked with emotion, Mike pulled a friend aside and said, "I need someone to listen to something I've never told *anyone* before. I don't even know if I can say it now. But I need someone to listen."

They sat silently in the car after the service, as many long minutes ticked by. Mike's friend prayed silently while Mike tried to put his memories into words. It started slowly at first, but then came gushing painfully out, faster and faster.

When Mike was just six years old, he had been sexually assaulted by a neighborhood bully. The teenager had lured him into a ditch and had forced him to remove all his clothes, then had bitten him severely on the penis. After this, he left with Mike's clothing. Mike was alone, naked and hurting, abandoned in a ditch like so much rubbish.

After many hours, a friend of Mike's sister found the dazed child still lying there and led him home. Many of the painful memories after that were still blocked, but Mike did remember being held all night long by his agitated parents. In spite of this, however, Mike recalls nothing that was ever done to bring the perpetrator to justice. His family never spoke of the matter after that.

That memory was so painful, says Mike, that it almost always stayed in the background, usually surfacing only in nightmares. Mike, for many years, believed that he had imagined the whole horrible thing.

Mike had never shared this pain with anyone because he felt somehow that the attack had been his fault, that he had deserved it in some way, or that he had deserved no better. His rocky marriages and self-destructive habits simply reinforced this deeply held belief.

But after coming to Christ, Mike began slowly and surely to recognize, at first in his head and then in his heart, his intrinsic worth to God. He was a unique human being, created in God's own image, worth saving and worth dying for. He wasn't simply trash to be discarded in a ditch, as he had believed all his life.

When Mike began to develop nonjudgmental relationships of mutual trust and transparency with other believers, this reinforced what he had been learning about his true value and identity. Eventually the time came when Mike felt it was safe to share his pain with someone else who would listen, to put his arm around Mike, to pray with him for healing, and to encourage him with words of affirmation.

That evening was the beginning of a process that continues to this day. Several more things have, since that time, come to the surface, including an additional molestation, this time by an older brother; and Mike's deeply repressed guilt about having forced his wife to have two abortions. A gentle man, Mike says, "I'm just grateful that the pattern of abuse never manifested itself through me to my children. I know that sometimes the temptation was there, but the Lord protected me from that without my even knowing it."

Mike has also come to understand a passion he has gained since coming to know the Lord for working with young men who have been similarly abused. He has befriended many young men and has led several support groups. Mike's son, who was at one time so addicted to drugs that many thought he would never survive, has come to know the Lord through his father's testimony and is an outstanding student and military officer. Mike is still dealing with many issues in his life, but he can point to a great deal of progress he has made in ten short years, as well as to ministry in the lives of others.

What were the conditions required for Mike to discover and begin healing from his own woundedness?

First and foremost, there were the *self-esteem* issues that he had to deal with. In most cases, woundedness remains hidden in our lives because we have adopted it, made it an innate part of our identity. It defines, in our own eyes, who we are and how we feel about ourselves.

Mike had to begin to release this false sense of identity to the Lord. He had to find his identity and security and value not in what he had done or where his life had taken him or what had happened to him, but in *who he was in the Lord's eyes*. When we begin to see ourselves as God sees us, we can then start to let go of our previous self-perceptions.

Second, Mike needed close, personal, and honest Christian *relationships*—people that he was praying with, people unafraid to ask probing questions, people concerned about his growth. He needed people who were praying for him and could understand when the Lord was beginning to do something with his life. He needed someone who knew him well enough and cared enough to sit quietly in the car and listen!

Third, Mike needed *confrontation.* He needed opportunities, like the church meeting that he had attended, where his memories and his conscience could be prodded until he came to the point where he was willing to recognize that there were painful issues that needed to be dealt with before he could progress further in his walk with the Lord. (This presupposes, of course, that he needed to recognize that his relationship with the Lord was a process of growth, with goals to be achieved and steps to be taken along the way.)

Fourth, Mike needed *confession.* There are two kinds of confession that are relevant here—confession to the Lord, in accordance with 1 John 1:9; and confession to other believers, in accordance with James 5:16. Mike recognized that he needed to break the silence. Any time there is a bondage issue in our lives, subtle but intense pressure will be exerted on the believer by the world, the flesh, and the devil to keep silent. Breaking that silence—in the right manner and time, and in the presence of the right people—is *always* a blow to Satan's agenda. Speaking out against personal bondage to woundedness is always difficult, but it always brings spiritual freedom.

Fifth, Mike needed *repentance.* True repentance involves a behavior adjustment or lifestyle shift—a turning from something, to something. Unhealthy habits must be replaced with healthy habits. We must "take off" the old man and "put on" the new. True repentance is not simply sorrow over sin; you can feel bad about indulging an appetite for pornography, but then continue in a lifestyle without canceling the subscriptions to *Playboy* and *Penthouse.* True repentance means canceling the subscriptions, refusing to walk down the street where the stores that sell the magazines are located, throwing out the TV set, and furthermore substituting a regimen of prayer, Bible study, and accountability to spiritual partners.

Sixth, Mike needed to *forgive.* He needed to forgive the person who had so deeply wounded him, and in so doing release the hold that that bitterness had over his life. Forgiveness doesn't minimize the sin; it's not saying "I'm okay, you're okay." It is unconditional. Forgiveness seeks reconciliation where possible but is even possible without personal reconciliation.

The seventh and final step is *service.* Confession, repentance, and forgiveness bring a great sense of relief, but these are only the beginning. We saw in John 9:3 that God sometimes has a purpose in our woundedness: that he might be glorified through the use of our lives to serve and free others from their woundedness. Not seeking to minister to the hurts of others, out of our own hurt, can cut short an intended blessing.

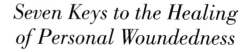

Seven Keys to the Healing of Personal Woundedness

- *Transfer of identity*—We must be made to see our value in the redeeming work of Christ
- *Building bridges*—Safe Christian relationships where mutual transparency and unconditional love is practiced
- *Confrontation*—Stimulating one another to actively confront issues of woundedness in our lives
- *Confession*—Turning over our sin and woundedness to God and to our Christian brothers and sisters
- *Repentance*—Turning from habits and lifestyles that necessitate sinful choices, to lifestyles and habits that please God
- *Forgiveness*—Forgiving unconditionally those who have wronged us, and seeking reconciliation where possible
- *Service*—Using our experience as a "wounded healer" to help free others with similar hurts

Discovering Unexpected Woundedness

Janet Logan was codirector of recovery ministries at Community Baptist Church of Alta Loma. Janet's focus in her position was originally on recovery groups for women who had been sexually, physically, or emotionally abused.

I had been praying about a possible ministry, praying that I would learn more and that God would open my eyes to see the needs. I heard the testimony of Debra, a woman in our church, about the abuse that she had suffered, and so I offered to be an intercessor for the recovery group that she was starting, called Tears of Joy. She let me in on the ground floor. At the time, I wasn't thinking of myself as wounded at all.

But during these recovery meetings, I gradually came to the realization that I *was* wounded. It was a bad experience in college, an attempted date rape. I realized as I participated in the group that this was a form of sexual abuse that I'd never dealt with, that had an impact on my life. The experience had been in my conscious memory, but I just hadn't paid much attention to it.

The Tears of Joy group had tapped into a real need in our church, and grew rapidly as a result. Soon it had seventeen members, and Janet says at that point they realized they needed to start another group. So she launched Tears of Joy II at one of CBC's daughter churches, New Song Church in Walnut. Janet led two cycles of the ten-week group, mentoring an apprentice leader as she did so.

Janet has started a number of different kinds of groups, following the same pattern—groups for managing anger, groups for overcoming fear, and groups for adult children of alcoholics. She identifies, recruits, and trains leaders on-the-job.

One advantage of the recovery-group structure is that it is fairly easy to raise up new leadership from within the ranks of those who participate in the groups. In addition, many groups are "scripted" so that much of the meeting can be "led" simply by reading through a text that has been prepared beforehand.

Jeanne Kirton leads recovery groups, under the auspices of Alternate Avenues Crisis Pregnancy Ministry in Ontario, California, for women who have suffered from the ill effects of abortion. A victim of abortion herself, Jeanne relates, "I was thrust into the role of leader when somebody put a workbook in my hands at the second meeting of a postabortion support group I attended several years ago. Basically all I did was read through the workbook exercises with the ladies, and God used that to do a tremendous work of healing in the group, primarily in me."

Jeanne follows the same process recommended by Janet Logan. At the beginning of each group, she prayerfully identifies an apprentice leader, then works closely with that woman throughout the thirteen-week course, gradually adding more responsibility until the woman she is working with is actually doing more of the up-front leading. Her apprentice is then ready to begin a second group, although Jeanne stays nearby to give ongoing support and consultation.

Uncovering the Pain in Your Church

Earlier we mentioned that rather than seeking to discover and understand the pain of others, too often we do the opposite—we attempt to ignore it, to allow it to remain hidden.

Many pastors who assert, "my church is healthy" would be very surprised to learn that there are great pockets of hidden pain in their churches. And we all know that a church body that does not feel the pain of its members is simply numb rather than healthy.

There are four steps to uncovering these pockets of pain in your church.

Listen. Listening must be both *passive* and *active.* Passive listening simply observes, but does so prayerfully. What are the issues of concern to the people in my church? What are they saying? What are the concerns behind what they are saying? If people are always praying for victory over the same sins, perhaps there is a pocket of woundedness there. If entire families, which ought to be (by virtue of their professions) making ends meet, are struggling financially, perhaps there are some recovery issues.

To listen passively, be sure you have plenty of opportunities for the people in your church to convey to you what is going on in their lives. Encourage members and friends alike to regularly jot comments about their lives in an appropriate section on their worship registration or response card. Take frequent opportunity to distribute blank note cards right in your worship services, asking members to list their praises and needs. Take the time to listen to all of your members, perhaps with an occasional telephone call to each home.

Active listening, on the other hand, seeks the answers to specific questions. Sometimes "anonymous surveys" to your church members, distributed with the worship bulletin and collected by ushers, can yield eye-opening results about what is *really* happening in your church—*if* the right questions are asked. Take time during the service for people to mark on their survey whether they or someone they love has experienced any of the problems listed. You will be amazed at the extent of problems within your church's ministry influence. (See appendix A for ideas to develop your own survey.)

Another way to listen actively is to seek the opinion of experts. What do psychologists or counselors in your church tell you about what Christians are going through emotionally? What can the physicians tell you about the stress-related diseases that are plaguing your members? What about the lawyers—what legal struggles are your people involved in? The financial advisors—what are the economic struggles? The employment counselors? The school advisors? The teachers? Figure out who the experts are, the people who are interacting daily with the lives of the people in your community, and ask them what people's needs are.

Relate. It sounds simplistic to say that a pastor should develop deeper relationships with specific individuals in the church. But too frequently a pastor of a church, because of the unique dynamics of being a pastor, simply doesn't have any friends in the church. Develop friendship relationships with individuals and use them, with their permission, as your ear to the church.

Debrief. Journalists and political pundits understand the value of exit polling. When dissatisfied people leave your church, they are making the statement: You can't help me anymore. Because they are not now so concerned about your ongoing friendship, they may be better able to speak frankly with you, telling you of their needs and concerns, than they were when they entered your church—*if* you ask them with humility, openness, candor, and a nonjudgmental attitude.

Investigate. What are the hurts in your community? If you can discover what they are, chances are, these hurts exist—if not to the same extent, then almost to that extent—within the four walls of your

Four Steps to Uncovering Pockets of Pain in Your Church

- Listen—both passively and actively
- Relate—build bridges with someone on the "inside"
- Debrief—conduct exit polling
- Investigate—discover the hurts of your community and consider their impact in your church

church. Do not assume that your church members are immune to the various ills that ail society. Expert observers point out that nearly all serious social problems including marital struggles, financial struggles, divorce, substance abuse, child abuse, sexual misconduct, abortion, and pornography, exist to the same extent among evangelical church members as they do among the nonchurched.

Passion Through Life Situation

Frequently people discover a passion for compassion gradually, as a result of their particular situation in life, and not necessarily because of a personal woundedness. Carole Clarke is a woman with a special heart for ministry, helping impoverished people in the Los Angeles area reclaim their dignity. Carole gained her passion for this kind of ministry during her long tenure as an executive vice-president with Lutheran Social Services. There she utilized and honed a talent for networking, uniting people to meet needs. She eventually left the organization due to some philosophical disagreements but retained the passion for ministry. Soon she found herself going solo and starting, in partnership with a small Baptist church in Hollywood, a ministry called Project Hope. The goal of Project Hope is to help people in an individualized way, one family at a time, gain the tools they need to overcome their own cycles of poverty and despair.

You may discover a hidden passion if you'll look carefully at what you have done and where you are.

After you have searched your life for personal woundedness, the next step is to *look where God has already placed you.* What is your vocation? How do you like to spend your time? What are your skills? Your hobbies? What type of ministry might your personality, your character, lead to? If you are the type of person who learns languages easily, is flexible in your personal standard of living and adapts easily, has no trouble making friends and relating to people from a different life situation than yourself, and has a strong gift of mercy, perhaps your well-suitedness for intercultural ministry is leading up to compassionate need-meeting in an urban setting.

In order to understand your suitability to a task, you have to understand yourself. How much time have you taken to look at your own strengths, gifts, skills, and character qualities? Knowing yourself is the first step to knowing how God has impassioned you to do ministry.

Passion Through Divine Call

And then there are those rare individuals who hear a voice, or find themselves struck blind by the side of the road.

Jonah is an interesting case because he is a man who received a prophetic call to ministry but was (at least at first) a study in lack of compassion. Here was a man with *absolutely no passion* to do ministry. Moreover, we have no indication that Jonah was equipped either by vocation, skills, character, or in any other way for his task. He was simply and inexorably called. And he responded to God by running in the opposite direction.

When God called Esther, through both her woundedness (as a member of an oppressed people) and her life situation (as queen), he did so gently. If she had declined the call, the result would simply have been, according to Mordecai, that God would have raised up deliverance from somewhere else, and that meanwhile she probably would have died along with other Jews.

Jonah, on the other hand, did say no. But God persisted, first through a storm that wouldn't quit, and then by giving Jonah a unique perspective of a fish's guts. Jonah was going to Nineveh, whether he wanted to or not!

So Jonah went to Nineveh, sulking all the way: "Forty more days and Nineveh will be overturned" (3:4). His compassion meter registered zero. No impassioned pleading with the Ninevites; Jonah simply didn't care. Let's call it *heartless obedience.*

Afterward, Jonah went to a place outside the city and sat down. No pleading with God on behalf of the city, like Abraham. No cries of "Wait, Lord! Withhold your hand! They're repenting!" No self-sacrificing gestures, like Moses. Jonah simply sat and waited for the city's destruction—which, of course, never came.

God had relented! He had seen the massive change of heart of the Ninevites, had had compassion on them, and had withheld his hand of judgment.

Jonah was appalled, and threw a temper tantrum. One gets the sense that his display of childish anger was the last straw for God, who decided then and there to do a work of heart-softening in Jonah's life. So, he caused a beautiful vine to grow up to shade Jonah from the rays of the sun. And then, just when Jonah was most enjoying its relief, God took it away. Jonah pouted and told God bitterly that he wanted to die. God's response was given as an object lesson to Jonah, and it shows his compassion for people:

> But the LORD said, "You have been concerned about this vine, though you did not tend it or make it grow. It sprang up overnight and died overnight. But Nineveh has more than a hundred and twenty thousand people who cannot tell their right hand from their left, and many cattle as well. Should I not be concerned about that great city?"
>
> *Jonah 4:10–11*

Jonah was specifically called by God to do ministry, and God used him after some trials and errors to accomplish what he wanted. But nearly as amazing as God's profound compassion for lost people was Jonah's lack of it. He saw people as problems, and not as people.

God, however, sees people as people! We are like children, who "cannot tell their right hand from their left." He even expressed compassion for the cattle! Why should they die needlessly?

The book of Jonah does not record the impact of this object lesson on Jonah's life, but one hopes he learned his lesson with humility.

The type of dramatic call issued to biblical characters like Jonah and Saul of Tarsus is still sometimes experienced by believers today. Church planter Dieter Zander got an advance peek at the church that God desired him to build, in a Paul-like vision, which he experienced as he was driving his car one day. Likewise, Robert Stratton, director of Church on the Street, says that his father received the calling for his ministry in Los Angeles as the result of a direct call from the Holy Spirit.

Sometimes, though, God issues a second type of divine call. It is a special glimpse from his heart for meeting a crucial need.

Larry Short tells of the beginnings of his own ministry, a pro-life equipping and crisis-pregnancy ministry called Project Jericho:

> One night I was driving home very late. I was alone in the car and was listening to a Focus on the Family broadcast by Dr. James Dobson. He was interviewing a medical doctor who was describing an ultrasound videotape taken of a fetus during an abortion procedure.

I had considered myself philosophically "pro-life" for a long time, and had even written an editorial in my college paper about it. But for me abortion had always been just another issue, and not one that I spent much time thinking about since it didn't really touch my life in a personal way.

But suddenly, listening to this fellow describing the video, I was picturing myself with that poor child in the womb, squirming and thrashing to avoid the sharp metal instruments of its destruction. All of a sudden I found I couldn't see the road ahead of me, and had to pull the car off to one side. I sat in that car and wept for a long time for that nameless child, so forgotten and alone. With a growing sense of horror I realized that the agony of this child must be just a small glimpse of what God himself lives through during each and every abortion. For surely, a compassionate God must be there, holding each child's hand in that dreadful moment of torment, and embracing him or her into the kingdom. With fifty million abortions per year worldwide, what a hellish assault this pain must be on the sovereignty of our Lord!

This was just the beginning of my "heartbreak education." As I started sharing my experience with people, I discovered to my surprise that some of them seemed personally insulted. One woman, a prayer warrior and a Bible-study leader at church, for whom I had the greatest respect, stopped talking to me and went out of her way to avoid me—which completely perplexed and baffled me.

About three months later this woman called me, and she was in tears. As I prayed and wept with her for several hours, she confessed to me the pain of two abortions she had had as a Christian teenager, and how destructive the effects of postabortion syndrome had been to her life. Only recently, for the first time in fifteen years, had she stopped having terrible nightmares about her lost children, but as soon as I told her about my experience she began having them again! That's why she'd stopped talking to me.

That confession was the beginning of a healing process in this woman's life, but it also opened the eyes of my heart to the pain suffered by abortion's second victim: the woman who feels she has no other choice but to terminate her pregnancy. I committed my life to doing everything I could to save women and children from that horrible fate.

Having your eyes opened to someone else's pain can be a very uncomfortable experience. What's more, you may instinctively know that what God is allowing you to experience will require a life response from you. Such a response will not be cheap; true compassion always costs. But, as Jonah discovered, to receive a call to ministry and then ignore or run away from it will cost, in the long run, much, much more.

The Rewards of Compassion

Can one person, finding God's assignment and working to complete it, make a difference? Are you throwing your life away by dedicating it to the service of others? Our attitude, as disciples, is to say yes once again to the Lord. Perhaps we will die poor and broken. But we know that if we refuse God and choose to live for ourselves, we will die anyhow, and we all exit this world with the same baggage we brought into it.

There is only one way to leave richer than we came. Paul says the result of our winning the race will be a "crown that will last forever" (1 Cor. 9:25). It is rewarded to those who:

- "Are strong," "teach others," "endure hardship," please our "commanding officer," and compete "according to the rules" *(2 Tim. 2:1–5)*
- "Long for his appearing," in order to receive the "crown of righteousness"*(2 Tim. 4:8)*
- "Persevere under trials," so that we may receive the "crown of life" promised to those who love God *(James 1:12)*
- "Shepherd God's flock," serving as overseers, not lording it over people but setting an example for them. "And when the Chief Shepherd appears, you will receive the crown of glory that will never fade away" *(1 Peter 5:2–4)*
- Are "faithful, even to the point of death"*(Rev. 2:10)*

It is important to realize what that crown consists of. In Philippians 4:1, Paul refers to his fellow believers, whom he has won, taught and ministered to as, "you whom I love and long for, my joy and crown." He tells the Thessalonians, "For what is our hope, our joy, or the crown in which we will glory in the presence of our Lord Jesus when he comes? Is it not you?" (1 Thess. 2:19).

Our crown is *people*—redeemed relationships! There are only three things that last forever—God, the Word of God, and the souls of women and men. The importance of relationships was the subject of Christ's parable of the shrewd manager, who upon losing his job as a rich man's manager created a future for himself by using his master's resources to win friends and influence people:

> The master commended the dishonest manager because he had acted shrewdly. For the people of this world are more shrewd in dealing with their own kind than are the people of the light. I tell you, use worldly wealth to gain friends for yourselves, so that when it is gone, you will be welcomed into eternal dwellings.
>
> *Luke 16:8–9*

What, in this context, is our worldly wealth? Clearly, it is not only our money, but our time, our energy, our talents, our attributes, and our gifts. God has given us these things as tools with which we may carry out our mission of reconciling people to him—building *redeemed relationships.*

Action Idea Checklist

- ☐ Ask God to cultivate a heart of compassion within you, and confirm your specific passion and calling.
- ☐ Deal with any unresolved areas of personal woundedness or recovery.
- ☐ Identify the kinds of woundedness in your church and in your community.
- ☐ Pray for God to raise up wounded healers who can facilitate a support group.
- ☐ Find appropriate, biblically based curriculum and develop a script to guide the facilitators.
- ☐ Launch one or more support groups.
- ☐ Network with other churches to meet a broader spectrum of needs.

Add your own follow-up items on the next page.

Contemplating the Power of a Listening Heart

There are three listening skills that you must develop after you have both a passion and a vision to minister:

- Listening to people with needs
- Listening to leaders who are seeking to meet those needs
- Listening to the Lord

They are all indispensable to true ministry. Each is both a *practice* and a *skill*. It is a *practice* in that you must intentionally set about to do it, and it can be done immediately and at any time if you set your mind and heart to it. And it is a *skill,* in that you can continually study its dynamics and learn to do it better.

These skills are not only mental skills, with techniques you can practice in order to do them more effectively, but they are heart skills as well. That is, you must direct your soul and spirit as well as your mind to the task of developing them. You must desire with your heart to do them, and to do them well. And you must depend on the Spirit of God to teach you to do them, for your spiritual perceptions as well as your mental perceptions will be employed.

These skills are not to be practiced sequentially, but concurrently. Review each of the three continually and practice them one within another. For example, while you are listening to the leaders to whom you have submitted yourself, you will be given opportunities to listen to needy people who are being assisted by that ministry. Simultaneously, in order to best come to understand people, you must be listening to the Lord as well.

Listening to People with Needs

Joni Eareckson Tada, the energetic woman whose courage in the face of near-total paralysis has inspired the nation, writes frequently of the serious disparity in the church's treatment of the disabled, which arises from our lack of empathetic listening. Millions of people in the U.S. are physically or mentally disabled.

- 8 thousand survive traumatic spinal-cord injury each year
- 420 thousand survive brain trauma each year
- 22 million have hearing impairments
- 2 million are deaf
- 220 thousand are totally blind
- 1.1 million are legally blind
- 8.2 million have visual impairments

In addition, there is tremendous ministry opportunity among the families of disabled people. The extent of the pain is evident. Four out of five marriages fail when one or more children in the family are disabled.

In spite of this wide open mission field, the church is doing very poorly at ministering to these individuals. A yearlong, intensive listening exercise conducted by Joni's ministry concluded that there is

a disturbing lack of sensitivity and alarming ineptitude within the church and the religious community in responding to the needs of the disability community.[1] Of primary concern was the issue of accessibility—not merely physical accessibility (parking for the disabled, cut curbs, ramps in entryways, widened and automatic doors, widened restroom stalls, audio amplification systems and interpreters for the hearing impaired, and tactile signs for the visually impaired), but "attitudinal accessibility" as well. Only one church in three has any sort of special ministry or program for any sort of disability. Joni tells a number of horror stories about how dysfunctional attitudes toward people who are disabled are manifested by the church—such as the man who was expelled from a church auditorium recently because a deacon was concerned about the tracks left by his wheelchair in the sanctuary's plush carpeting.

As a result, people with disabilities are frequently highly disillusioned with Christianity. Observers note that about four out of five families that include a disabled member who have attended church don't return because they experience some form of rejection by that church. Joni says that able-bodied people fear people with disabilities and reject them for three reasons—because they don't understand them, they don't know what to do or how to help them, and helping them is simply not a priority. Only one in twenty disabled people currently attend church, and fewer than three in twenty have professed Christ as Savior.

The sad thing about this is that reaching out to people with disabilities doesn't have to be a complex or expensive proposition. Joni points out that there are many simple things that can be done, things within the capacity of every church. For instance, Crossroads Christian Church in Corona, California, has a program called Save Our Sanity, which provides loving care for the children, both disabled and able-bodied, of families that have a member who is disabled, so that the moms can get out on a Saturday morning once a month and go shopping or do any other activity for relaxation and "escape." A similar program, called Mother's Day Out is conducted by the First Evangelical Free Church of Fullerton, California. Other churches have somewhat more complex programs, such as an annual week-long getaway retreat for families with disabilities.

Churches who listen to people with disabilities, and to their families, have realized that one of the biggest needs of these families is what JAF Ministries calls respite care—the opportunity for family members to take a break from the struggles of caring, day in and day out, for people with disabilities. And this is a simple need that can be easily provided for by any church with caring people.

Stephen Covey relates that the ability to listen empathetically is the single most important principle of interpersonal communications. We may consider that those with whom we relate have set up an unspoken ground rule: "Unless you're influenced by my uniqueness, I'm not going to be influenced by your advice."[2]

We're filled with our own rightness, our own autobiography. We want to be understood. Our conversations become collective monologues, and we never really understand what's going on inside another human being.[3]

Our natural tendency, when thrust into an urban setting, or any other one where people are hurting, is to apply our own auto-biographies to these people's problems. We're not thinking of them as unique individuals who desire to be understood; we're simply thinking of them as *problems to be fixed.* Out of our own rightness (after all, we're not stuck in the same situation they are) we pre-scribe our solution for them. Meanwhile, these individuals are not so much looking for solutions to their problems as they are broad-casting to us their desire to be affirmed, to be valued as unique, to be *understood.*

Covey says that empathetic listening "diagnoses before it prescribes."

> Suppose you've been having trouble with your eyes and you decide to go to an optometrist for help. After briefly listening to your complaint, he takes off his glasses and hands them to you.
>
> "Put these on," he says. "I've worn this pair of glasses for ten years now and they've really helped me. I have an extra pair at home; you can wear these."
>
> So you put them on, but it only makes the problem worse.
>
> "This is terrible!" you exclaim. "I can't see a thing!"
>
> "Well, what's wrong?" he asks. "They work great for me. Try harder."
>
> "I am trying," you insist. "Everything is a blur."
>
> "Well, what's the matter with you? Think positively."
>
> "Okay. I positively can't see a thing."
>
> "Boy, are you ungrateful!" he chides. "And after all I've done to help you!"[4]

Here in Los Angeles, there is a secular pop psychologist who has a call-in TV show. For an hour each day, he sits and listens. People describe bizarre sexual fetishes and generally spill their angst.

The man obviously has a great deal of wisdom and discernment. And he needs it, because the problem is—and this is possibly owing to the nature of the medium—he doesn't have much time in which to make a diagnosis and prescribe a cure that will wow the viewers. In any given one-hour show, he may talk to a dozen different callers. He doesn't suffer fools gladly—if they don't get right to the point, he whips them into line with a well-placed jab or witticism.

He furrows his brow and listens intently for as long as he dares, asking a few crucially placed questions along the way. But all of a sudden, the person's entire life and problems have fallen into place, and he assaults them with the solution.

Sometimes the solution seems to fit (he *is* good), but always, it seems, the people on the other end are left sort of breathless and half-satisfied, unsure of how they should *feel* about the encounter. Why? The pop-psychology guru has given them a hearing of a full five minutes, and now he feels like he knows them. One gets the feeling he's finished listening. He's made his rapid-fire diagnosis, followed it with a rapid-fire prescription, and boom, now all they have to do is follow his instructions.

What's lacking in this whole scenario is not the listening. The doc is doing a good job of that in the two or three minutes he has allotted to it. He's listening intently, filtering the person through his lenses. Perhaps he is eliminating the options one by one—*psychopath? No. Paranoid schizo? Nope. Obsessive-compulsive? Not. Ah, here it is. Classical Freudian case of mother love. Haven't had one of those in a while.* Diagnosis made. He pulls a prescription out of the hat, and it's on to the next call before an objection can be made.

What's lacking is listening that's agenda-free. Listening without the interpretive lenses. Listening in order to truly understand—to know and to come to empathize with—the other person.

There's power in listening to people with needs. There is a more intensive form of listening that is called "incarnational ministry" by those who practice it. Just as Christ "incarnated" or came to dwell among us, so those who practice this type of ministry seek to dwell in the midst of the people among whom they minister. Ray Bakke realized, early on in his ministry, that if he were to be a true urban pastor, he must *live among* those whom he ministered to, much like his historical mentor, Charles Simeon, who at the turn of the eighteenth century shocked his well-to-do Cambridge congregants by opening his church and his life to the poor people who filled the crumbling hovels in the back streets of the city. Thus, since 1960 when his ministry began, Bakke has lived with his family very visibly in rented apartments in "bad neighborhoods" of inner-city Chicago.

John Hayes is another outstanding example of incarnational ministry. As director of InnerCHANGE with Church Resource Ministries, John and his wife Deanna live in an apartment among Asian refugee-immigrants in Long Beach, California. John's special brand of what he calls "presence ministry" first became evident to us when we visited him at his former residence on Minnie Street in Santa Ana several years ago.[5] John reflects: "Presence ministry breaks down barriers. It ministers face-to-face. It knows people by name. It's a good thing, too, because God knows us by name. In his kingdom, there will be neither Jew nor Greek, Black nor White. Heaven is strictly a first-name-basis kind of place."

John Perkins, the founder of Voice of Calvary Ministries and most recently the Harambee Center in Pasadena, California, has been living since the fifties in the communities where God has called him to minister—some of the most impoverished and violent places in America. He calls his own brand of presence ministry *relocation.* "You can't disciple people unless you have a community relationship, unless you're living with them." Relocation is "bringing the people of God back into the community of need, where they can make that need their own. We seek to address the physical and economic needs of the community by being God's people here in this neighborhood and looking out for the well-being of the people, especially the youth." John says their most important role is "parenting—it's what's missing in this community. That's why it's so important that we be here, that we live here in this neighborhood. To be able to hug and kiss these kids is one of the most important things that could happen in our lives."

Whether it's called incarnational ministry, relocation, or presence ministry, the need for this type of ministry seems to have so often escaped our missions endeavors of the past, marked by missions compounds (offering the home-style amenities that one might miss by truly living among the natives) and missionaries sending their kids out of the country for a "real" education. But it is this powerful principle that was a common thread woven throughout our journey to various urban ministries in different cities across the United States. Glen Kehrein, director of Circle Urban Ministries in downtown Chicago, lives with his family in a thoroughly urban neighborhood only a mile away from the combination mission and church where he works and worships. Almost every week Circle brings a team of young people, from a suburban church, into the inner city to live and work for a week, but mostly to simply get to know the people.

"Too often," Glen says, "Christians approach the inner city like an assignment, a project. They come with an idea of the ministry or the service they are going to do here. But we encourage them instead to come with an open mind and heart, to listen to the people who live here, to get to know them first. You can't really meet someone's needs until you come to understand who they are."

Such a willingness, Glen says, changes perspective and changes lives. "When they first arrive, they're nervous and hesitant. The week seems like a long time. But by the week's end, they've made some friends, developed some relationships." Glen couldn't remember anyone who hadn't wanted to stay longer. Many of them do, working for a year or longer as an intern for Circle before going out to other urban areas on longer term missions assignments of their own.

Covey asserts that, "next to physical survival, the greatest need of a human being is psychological survival—to be understood, to be affirmed, to be validated, to be appreciated." This is a principle that many successful prostitutes understand. Their customers come to them ostensibly for a sexual thrill, but their primary need may instead be for someone to listen to them and understand them.

If a real and primary need of the people to whom we minister is indeed to be understood—if that need is perhaps on a par with whatever other physical needs we believe they might have, their disability, their hunger, their homelessness, or their poverty—then simply in the act of listening empathetically we have made what Covey calls "a deposit in their psychological bank account." We have ministered to them before we have even started to minister to them. We have gained trust and established that we are "safe," and they can share their needs and feelings with us.

Listening empathetically to others leads us to realize another facet of ministry—it is a two-way process.

Carl George, Director of the Charles E. Fuller Institute of Church Growth in Pasadena, California, has said, "Help is not help unless it is perceived to be helpful." People cannot truly be helped unless and until they have come to the point when they are willing to *respond* to the person who is offering to help them.

At the Last Supper, Christ girded himself with a towel and took a basin of water with which to wash the apostles' feet. When he came to Peter, the fisherman objected strenuously, "No, you shall never wash my feet." Christ gave Peter a clear choice. "Unless I wash you, you have no part with me." That changed things quickly for our talk-before-you-think friend. Suddenly he was willing to be served (John 13:8–9).

God never forces his help on us. If he did, then—because of his compassionate nature—there would probably not be any suffering. But we could never be free moral agents, made in the likeness of God, without our having the innate ability to refuse God's help and say no to his requests.

As agents of God's compassion, this is a principle we must learn to accept:

First, we must till the soil by asking God for fertile and receptive hearts. God ripens the fruit; ask him to help you work with fruit that is ripe for the picking. Ask for guidance and for spiritual discernment.

Second, we must put off any prideful, arrogant attitudes that we might bring with us into an interaction with a person to whom we are seeking to minister. We must ensure the purity of our motive. Are we approaching the person because we desire honestly to be obedient to God and express his love toward others in service? If so, we must recognize the uniqueness and the value of the person to whom we are seeking to minister, whether that person is a back-alley drunk or the prime minister of England. We must be willing to approach him with the desire to understand rather than the desire to be understood (and admired).

Third, we must *earn* a hearing among those to whom we would minister, by approaching them first as an empathetic listener. Such an attitude says: "You are an important and valuable person to God and to me. I want to get to know you, to understand you and value you for who you are. If there is a way I can serve you, I want to learn what it is, but I respect you enough to leave you alone if that's what you really want."

Charles Simeon, whose pastoral ministry in early eighteenth-century London served as a model for Ray Bakke's urban ministry in Chicago, exemplified this type of approach. His first step as pastor was to go and visit with the poor and dispossessed of the community around the church, spending time getting to know them and asking, "How may I be of service to you?" In this endeavor he was opposed by many of the Christians in the congregation he had been assigned to pastor. Yet he continued to show honor to the poor, and after a number of years the hearts and minds of even the most staid members of his church began to soften.

Fourth, we must be willing to be *ministered to* by the person with whom we are developing the listening relationship. This means we must exercise trust and exhibit some vulnerability. In any human relationship there is the unavoidable possibility of betrayal; Christ's dealings with Judas demonstrate to us that we must be willing to accept this possibility.

Fifth, we must have an accurate view of how we can help. Too often we are unrealistic in our own estimation of our abilities or our capacity to be of assistance. We must understand the value of helping in simple ways before we propose complex schemes. We should not promise the sun when we can only deliver the moon.

And finally, we must be willing at some point to let go, to release. True service never develops dependency; it always develops people. True service disciples another; that is, it seeks to understand the extent to which a person has the capacity to stand alone, and then develops him to the limits of that capacity. If possible it seeks to bequeath to another individual the human dignity of saying: "I believe that, with sufficient training, you can do this by and for yourself."

Listening to the Leaders Doing Compassion Ministry

One thing you can bet on, and that is the truth of Christ's admonition in John 4:35: "I tell you, open your eyes and look at the fields! They are ripe for harvest." In a hurting world, ministry opportunities abound. When you set out to compassionately meet human needs, the likelihood that you will run out of things to do is remote indeed.

Yet, it does not make sense to try to reinvent the wheel. You can save yourself a lot of time and trouble by learning from the mistakes and successes of others who have gone before you. For example, you may discover, through your research, that another ministry is already functioning effectively, meeting the needs of your target group. There is much you can learn from others who are already doing what you sense God wants you to do. To learn, you need to engage in a second phase of listening: *listen to the leaders doing compassion ministry.*

Finding the Leaders

After coming to know the needs of the people in an area of ministry where you have been impassioned to work, the next step is to set out to discover what is already being done, and how it is being done. In order to do this, you must play the role of detective, tracking down those who are already engaged in ministry similar to the one that you envision, and seeking to learn from them.

Who are these individuals? Start in your church by talking with your pastor or someone who is in touch with ministries being conducted by various individuals in the church. Describe the people that the Lord is drawing you to minister to, and ask who else might be doing ministry in this area. If no one knows who is ministering, ask who might know. Then expand the scope of your search beyond your own church. Call other ministering churches in the area and inquire of them in the same manner. (Be sure to write down all contact persons who prove to be helpful in answering your questions. This beginning network of relationships may become very valuable to you later on.)

You may also wish to consult local, public sources of information. In the beginning of many telephone books can be found a section listing the phone numbers of agencies who deal with or refer to various emergency or social services. Some may also include an abbreviated national 800 directory with "hotlines" or "social services" sections. Many of these agencies may be able to make referrals to the type of organization you seek.

Another way to discover existing need-meeting organizations or persons might be to talk to the people in your target group. Ask them: Where have you gone for help in the past? Who are the people who have been of assistance to you? Do you have friends who have been helped by a minister or an agency?

Meeting the Leaders

Once you have determined who the people (if any) are who are already meeting needs within your target group, the next step is meeting them and learning about their efforts. If this group is associated with another church, you may wish to pay that church a visit. If the need-meeting agency is a group within the church, find out when and where they meet and who the leaders are. Then call and explain that you are seeking information on their ministry. With the dual goals of learning about their ministry and helping them to serve the people whose needs they are meeting, ask if you can observe. Very few groups that are seeking to meet needs will turn away offers of volunteer help, though some may ask you for a commitment of time.

If, after a preliminary visit, the ministry looks like something that could be mutually beneficial (could help you learn about the ministry you have selected as well as give you an opportunity to serve effectively and meet the needs of your target group), make yourself available to the leaders as an apprentice. Do not despise whatever training they offer, but complete it faithfully, attentively, and patiently.

In our observations of ministry leaders we have concluded that the vast majority are: (1) very busy people, but (2) very generous people. They will seek to invest their time where they feel it will pay off for their ministry. If they see you as a serious, qualified seeker trying to understand how to minister to the people, and if they are good leaders, then they will selflessly invest in you whatever time and energy is required to train you to assist them in this task. In fact, as Fred Smith has said, "A leader is not a person who can do the work better than his followers; he is a person who can get his follower to do the work better than he can."[6]

There is no better way to receive an education in serving a particular target group than by joining a ministry led by a true leader who understands the value of effectively training volunteers. If you find such persons, God has blessed you with a valuable resource; submit yourself to them without reservation.

The Mind-set of an Apprentice

As an apprentice to a leader of your target ministry, keep these principles in mind:

You are there both to serve and to learn. You have made a commitment before the Lord to minister to hurting people. Ask him to bring you such people through the auspices of the ministry or leader you are now apprenticing under. Ask the Lord to effectively develop your ministry and your ministry skills within that framework. Within the parameters established by the leadership of this ministry, take the initiative to explore, to experiment, to listen. Try it their way; and try it your way to the extent that you are given license to do so. Keep a journal for later review of everything that you are learning.

Your passion is valuable. You have specific ideas about how to serve and about which you have become excited. Those ideas may or may not fit within the framework in which God has now placed you to learn and minister. To the extent that they fit, try them out. But to the extent that you are not given license to use differing methods, hold back until a time when you are given the freedom to test them.

Recognize, however, that just because you have not been given license by the leadership of the ministry under which you are apprenticing to field-test your own ideas does not mean that they are not valuable or that they are not from the Lord. Like Moses, be patient and wait for a time when you can exercise the passion the Lord has given you in the way that he directs. Be open, meanwhile, to the possible benefits of other people's methods. They have, after all, a similar passion to your own, and more experience in working with it.

Seek the blessing and anointing of your leadership. Help them to understand that you will never be in competition with them, but desire only to help them fulfill their goals. There may come a day when you move out from under their authority, but hopefully it will be with their blessing and support.

Developing a network of mentors and advisors, under whom you have ministered and with whom you have established healthy and positive relationships, is one of the most valuable resources you will ever establish as a leader. It will benefit you and your ministry for years to come.

If the leadership to whom you have submitted yourself is godly and skilled leadership, they will recognize your potential as a leader and, when the time is right, bless and release you for the task to which God has called you. True leadership never seeks to stifle or horde; it always seeks to develop and send. There will come a day when they will say, "I have taught you all that I am able, and learned from you besides. Now, I am releasing you to go and develop the ministry that God has impassioned you to develop."

Listening to the Lord

The third and most important listening skill is the skill of listening to the Lord. Like the first two listening skills—listening to hurting people and listening to leaders doing compassion ministry— it is not sequential, but must be practiced in tandem with the other two. It is, in one sense, the first skill, the middle skill, and the last skill.

It has been said, "You can never be too prepared." But sometimes, in the midst of our human activities, we can be too confident in our education, too dependent on the comprehensiveness of our preparations. There are, however, always the unexpected elements, the unprepared for, the incalculable factors. There will always arise tests and demands that are outside of the realm of our best laid plans and preparations for coping. Stephen Covey says that in order to deal with such contingencies, we must operate not on the basis of plans, but on the basis of an internal compass. That compass, he says, will be the set of principles and our commitment to them that lie at the center of our universe—what he calls "natural law."

The Christian takes this a step further, acknowledging and affirming that at the center of our center—the source of our principles— lies the eternal and abiding person of God. Our "compass" is the revealed Word of God, the principles set forth in Scripture, applied to our lives by the work of the Holy Spirit.

To acknowledge this truth is to affirm that we are, and must remain, fully dependent on God and his revelation of himself. It is not enough to simply take a class in God's will and then proceed, on your own, without a look back over your shoulder. Each of us must be involved in continuing education. We will, for the rest of our earthly lives, and probably for the rest of eternity as well, ever be coming to know God; we must ever be sitting at his feet and learning of him. We must ever be asking him to expand the size of our cup as well as to continue filling it up.

The implication of this truth is that listening to the Lord will be our most important practice and activity.

Listening to the Lord: Prerequisites

Entire volumes have been written on this subject. But we will briefly summarize here the most important principles. There are two aspects to listening to the Lord—*prerequisites* and *practices*. First we will look at the three prerequisites to listening to the Lord.

An attitude of obedience. Only disciples can sit at the feet of the Lord and learn from him. A disciple is a learner, one who is willing to be taught. We have seen that God never forces himself on us; if we are unwilling to receive from him, he will not give to us. The attitude of a disciple is an attitude of trust, one that says, "Yes, I will follow you. I will spend the time sitting at your feet. I will be taught. Because I trust you to do what is best, I will obey what you command, even when it is difficult."

Meditation on what he has already told you. It is foolish to say "I am ready to listen to the Lord," if you have already chosen not to listen to what he has already tried to tell you. Moreover, a part of that active listening process is seeking out what God has already said to us through his Word, "I have hidden your word in my heart that I might not sin against you" (Ps. 119:11). Meditating on his precepts is preventive medicine against the onslaught of sin. And, as we shall see in the next point, it is sin itself that prevents us from hearing his voice.

Uprightness of heart. Psalm 66:18–19 says, "If I had cherished sin in my heart, the Lord would not have listened; but God has surely listened and heard my voice in prayer." God's righteousness comes through faith in Jesus Christ to all who believe; there is no difference among humans, since we all have sinned and have fallen short of the glory of God. We are all justified freely by his grace, through the redemption that came by Christ's atoning act (Rom. 3:22–24). Compared to God, our hearts are hopelessly impure. The good news is that he has imputed his righteousness to us.

Walking in purity of heart is a day-by-day, moment-by-moment proposition. It means keeping your conscience fresh and sensitive, and never choosing to ignore it. It means remaining always in an attitude of prayer and searching yourself courageously and vigilantly. And it means applying 1 John 1:9–10 whenever you come up against any obstacle that has introduced new impurity into your heart that thereby hinders your ability to listen to the Lord.

Listening to the Lord: Practices

The following steps are in a category of activities that are simple to suggest but difficult to do.

Daily time with the Lord. Christ placed premium value on his time for meditation and prayer. When he was pressed by crowds and a heavy agenda, he sought solitude and sacrificed such personal physical necessities as sleep and food in order to prioritize his time and spend enough of it with his Father.

This time with the Lord may be unstructured, at least at times, but most of us need the discipline a structure imposes. Many people have presented their ideas for a structured time with the Lord. It usually includes structured prayer (and there are many ideas on how to do this), Bible study, meditation and/or memorization, and often keeping a journal. We live in an age where you can go to your local Christian bookstore and obtain a wide variety of books that will help you find the structure that is best for you in maintaining your personal discipline. Dallas Willard's book *The Spirit of Discipline* provides an excellent resource for the variety of ways to deepen your spiritual intimacy with God.[7]

Setting spiritual goals. Our listening relationship with the Lord will be a living and growing thing. It will be a process.

As in all processes, it must be broken up into doable components, into bite-sized pieces with achievable goals and places for rest and celebration along the way. This is a principle well understood by mountain climbers, who say that although they set their ultimate sights on the peak and cherish the periods of ascent, they really live for the ledges. Tobin Sorenson was considered one of the three best alpinists in the world (alpinism is that specific and very challenging category of mountain climbing in which one uses certain techniques to make vertical ascents on ice- and snow-covered rock faces). He conquered many of the world's most difficult peaks, including an extremely challenging and dangerous solo, midwinter speed climb of the Matterhorn.

Tobin said he praised God for the ledges. They were his "signposts" along the way. A ledge meant accomplishment—you had completed another step in the journey to the top. They were places of rest and revitalization. An experienced climber can actually pin himself to a vertical face and get a full night of sleep in that position; but a ledge always means an added measure of relaxation and refuge.

Does your spiritual journey have a peak—an ultimate objective? Perhaps just as important, does it have easily identified ledges along the way? Is the distance between these ledges realistic and crossable? Are the ledges substantial enough to provide a foothold for rest, a celebration of achievement, a refuge from the occasional and unexpected storms of life?

Periodic evaluation. The so-called mid-life crisis has come to be one of the most celebrated phenomena of American culture, particularly but not exclusively among men. And when you boil down the essence of what a mid-life crisis typically is, it is a *forced evaluation—usually the result of circumstances beyond one's control (like aging or the emptying of one's family nest)—of the direction, meaning, and accomplishments of one's life.* Observers agree that the most effective way to prevent a serious mid-life crisis is to short-circuit this forced evaluation by building in a series of more intentional, and more easily accomplished, evaluations along the way. In other words, don't allow yourself to be surprised by the lethal combination of an ill-defined purpose and a lack of evaluation of your effectiveness!

Strategically plan for periodic sessions of intense evaluation and personal reflection.

Larry Short, who attended Biola University (a private evangelical institution in La Mirada, California) relates how this discipline became established in his life:

> Much to my surprise, I did learn a few things at school. Professor, accomplished writer, and media expert Dr. Lowell Saunders, to whom I owe a great deal, taught a summer session that I will never forget, entitled Writing for Personal Enrichment. In that brief class we gained several very important skills, including writing poetry as a catharsis, understanding ourselves through the exploration of childhood memories, and writing letters to God as a method of intimate communication with the Ultimate. But perhaps the most valuable and enduring skill was that of preparing an "annual report." Doc taught us how to prepare a sort of state-of-the-union or corporate-style report to the stockholders of "Me, Inc." In it, we identified our stockholders (family members, fellow churchmen, friends, and business colleagues who have an "investment" in our development), summarized on a "balance sheet" our personal "assets and liabilities," evaluated our progress toward past goals, and affirmed them or established new ones. It was suggested that we take at least an entire day of solitude, if not two or three, to go through this process, and that we do it once a year at a key time of the year.
>
> I adopted the week after New Year's Day for this process, which has worked out very well with my schedule. It is a time when my energy is fresh and my enthusiasm for the future is at a peak. My lifestyle is such that enduring habits are few. In one form or another, I have managed to prepare this annual report every year since taking that class, about thirteen years ago. Very rarely do I share anything but portions of the final product with others; it is between the Lord and me, a fact that gives me a great deal of freedom to be honest about my needs and weaknesses. Although preparing this report can be a gut-wrenching exercise, I have found few things that have contributed equal value to my productivity and sense of personal satisfaction over the years.

Listening to the Lord: Intercessors

King David, known as a "man after God's own heart," lived his life on the edge but lived it very close to the heart of God. He was a man who knew the meaning of worship. He danced, without prideful concern for the thoughts of others, joyfully before the ark of the covenant as it was returned to Jerusalem. He penned hundreds of psalms that demonstrated his grasp of moment-by-moment worship of the Almighty. One would think that if any man were able, on his own accord, to understand God's heart and hear his voice, it would be David.

But the Scripture also paints, at the same time, an almost schizophrenic, dualistic picture of the other "dark" side of this great king. We are shocked to read of David's sordid affair with Bathsheba, in the midst of all God's blessings, and of the sexual sin, deceit, lying, callousness, and even brutal murder of a loyal follower that it led to.

We understand how difficult and consuming it is to continue unrepentant in grievous sin for hours, days, or even weeks. But David continued, unrepentant, in his guilt after these grievous sins with Bathsheba for an entire year!

An entire year had passed before David was approached by an intercessor, the prophet Nathan. Nathan confronted David with his sin in a very dramatic fashion (*"Thou art the man!"*) and it was almost as if a light went on in this great king's head. Without offering excuses or rationalizations, he immediately fell on his face and cried, "I have sinned against the Lord." Just as quickly, Nathan replied, "The Lord has taken away your sin. You are not going to die." But then he proceeded to detail the physical consequences of David's sin against the Lord—God's judgment of Israel (see 2 Sam. 11–12).

But the natural question for David is this: How on earth could a man who was considered a friend of God, who had walked so closely with the Lord all his life, be so blind to the way he had injured and grieved God that he could persist in his unrepentance for an entire year? Why did it take Nathan the prophet to point out to David the error of his ways? Why couldn't such a great man figure this out for himself?

This is just one of many biblical illustrations of the fact of our interdependence as believers. God did not create us to walk through the Christian life alone. We were made to function as a part of a team. We each have blind spots. Another person is able to perceive our blind spots easily, but they elude us totally. This is why great men and women of God, who have walked with him for years and have studied the Bible endlessly, can crash so abruptly and totally.

The point is: We need one another. Any ministry endeavor will only be as strong as the team that supports it. A team of intercessors should be the first building block of any new ministry endeavor. As new churches are planted in America and abroad by today's new breed of missionaries, these prayer teams are frequently the first unit around which the rest of the church is built.

Recruit your team of intercessors similar to the way in which you would recruit a team of financial supporters. Ask for individuals who share your vision and are willing to make a solid commitment to support your passion in regular, focused prayer, for a limited period of time, like one year.

Your best intercessors will be those with a passion for intercession. But also seek to mobilize a team that reflects a diversity of gifts, skills, personalities, vocations, and other characteristics. Keep, for their sake, a complete accounting of prayer needs and answered prayers, and share regular reports with them. Pray with them regularly but encourage them as well to gather and pray when you are not present.

The presence of a team of intercessors not only establishes your accountability to the body of Christ but acknowledges the important truth that God speaks to us through his Word, through personal prayer, through meditation, through worship, and also through the gifts and abilities of other members of the body. Establishing this pattern of interdependence early in your ministry will keep you in good stead later when you face the successes and the obstacles that are bound to come your way.

Keep on Listening

As we hinted at the beginning of this chapter, the development of listening practices and skills, and the cultivation of a listening heart, are not simply a patch of ground that must be traversed in the process of building your ministry. They are, rather, an ongoing process of life that must be practiced and refined as long as you continue to minister to others—which will hopefully be until the day you die. Keep coming back again and again to these principles, for they are central to your ability to build relationships and minister to the needs of others. Listening—to hurting people, to leaders of compassion ministries, and to the Lord—is not optional for those who would see the kingdom of God established in their midst.

Action Idea Checklist

- ☐ Ask God to help you understand people better through empathetic listening, hearing both content and feelings.
- ☐ Identify one potential ministry focus group; listen extensively to discover their needs and how to help meet those needs. Conduct interviews with several people to gain deeper understanding of: (1) individuals who have need, (2) family members, (3) experienced ministry leaders, and (4) social service workers.
- ☐ Serve as an apprentice in a ministry area where you can learn and grow.
- ☐ Cultivate spiritual disciplines to deepen your relationship with God and increase your capacity to listen to the Holy Spirit.
- ☐ Build an intercessory team to support and encourage you through prayer; communicate at least monthly with them.
- ☐ Evaluate your church's physical and attitudinal accessibility; make changes to reach out to people with disabilities.

Add your own follow-up items below.

4

Calling Together an Impassioned Team

There are rare moments in history when God does his work through one person—usually a prophet like Elijah—called out to bear witness against a society travelling in the wrong direction. But in the vast majority of cases in the kingdom of God, teamwork is everything. God accomplishes ministry through diverse gifted people working together for a common purpose.

After first answering the question, Why Teams? this chapter will get down to the nuts and bolts of:

- How do you clarify a team vision that will help recruit and motivate potential team members?
- Where do you find those members, and how do you present that vision to them?
- How do you understand your own role, as well as the roles of the team's various members, and how you will interact together?
- How do you train your team members?
- How do you effectively delegate ministry?
- How will your ministry team relate to the local church?

Why Teams?

Christ created us and knew that we were not meant to work alone. There are rare examples of Christians throughout history, like Hudson Taylor, who began work alone in pagan societies to accomplish God's purposes. Their missionary efforts had the special touch of God on them. But even then, these men and women as quickly as they were able always built a team among the people to whom they ministered.

The fact is, we need one another! We alluded, near the end of chapter 3, to some of the reasons for this:

- Our *blind spots* require that we be in close connection with people who can protect us from the results of our tunnel vision.
- We are given *diverse gifts and talents* as resources with which to conduct ministry. The effective team, and it alone, contains the entire complement of these gifts and talents necessary to complete the assignment it has been given.
- We need to support one another in *faithful prayer*. We need the power of a team of intercessors who are calling down heaven on our behalf.

In addition, there are many other important reasons for building an impassioned team:

- Individual humans burn out and get discouraged. We need our team in order to *buoy us up* when times are tough.
- Being a part of an impassioned team helps provide desperately needed *meaning* and a *sense of belonging* to our lives.
- The *interdependency* of being a part of a team teaches us valuable lessons about our humanity. It teaches us humility, patience, and how to love.
- An effectively functioning team, with the diverse perspectives of its various members focused on the achievement of a goal, will experience *synergy*—that is, the whole will be greater than the sum of its parts. Teams have their own unique *identity*, which is something greater than simply the sum of the personalities of the team's members.
- But, perhaps most importantly to mortal human beings who "fade as the grass," teams are the only effective way to create a ministry effort that is *enduring and reproducible*.

Building a Team: The First Steps

Bear Valley Church in Lakewood, Colorado, with twenty special target-group ministries, is famous for its ministry teams. One of the first questions they ask people who approach them with a vision for ministry is, "Who have you found who shares your vision and is willing to work alongside you on this?"

Clarify Your Team Vision

It's one thing to understand a vision for ministry, and another to be able to articulate it effectively so that others will "catch" it.

And that is the essence of the challenge. Vision cannot simply be cognitively understood, although that is the first step. Beyond merely grasping the meaning of a vision, people's hearts must be engaged to value that vision and accept it as their own. This is a two-step process:

Having your heart broken by things that break the heart of God. This is the first step of compassion. We must become aware of human need in such a way that God uses that perception to break our hearts.

Understanding the facts about a problem is the smallest of the two challenges that confront the person who desires to share his or her vision with others. It must also be our goal to help our brothers and sisters open their hearts to be broken by the pain of the wounded. How do we do this?

First is *prayer*. There is one alone who is able to work unseen in the hearts of people, and it is to him we must first appeal. We must pray specifically and ceaselessly for those we desire to join our team, that their hearts would be fallow ground to be broken by the pain by which our hearts have been broken.

Second is *observation*. We must take these people to where the need is (or else bring the need to them), to allow them to see it for themselves. And we must encourage them to respond to it openly, as unto God.

Comprehending how this need can be met by strategic acts of Christian compassion. It is not simply enough to have compassion. The compassion of Christ is always followed by action. Do we have a realistic and workable action plan that will help to meet the need at hand? Can people see that it will work, and will do so in a manner that will not waste anyone's time, effort, or expense?

People who are open to the leading of the Holy Spirit, whose hearts have been broken by the need, will jump readily on your bandwagon when they see that your ideas present a real and present opportunity for meeting that need.

Plan Your Approach

You have already established a passion for reaching out to a certain target group of people. A mistake we commonly make in team building is building a team of outsiders who are not acquainted with those in our target group. They have not lived among them, sharing their burdens and heartaches. Too often we build a team that looks too much like we do.

Instead, we ought to focus on walking among the people to whom we desire to minister, drawing our impassioned team from their midst.

This may not be an easy thing to do—you'll have to ask yourself the right questions, and proceed with vigor and determination. First, identify within your church or other churches in your community the constituencies of believers who most closely represent the target group that you wish to reach. If your passion is to reach out to people with disabilities and to their families, search for those individuals who may have firsthand experience with disability, either personally or through someone they know. These are the individuals among whom you ought to spend your time.

Walk Among the People

Second, begin to "walk among" these people. Discover the groups in which they circulate, and make yourself a part of them. Participate in their activities. Find out what they do for recreation, and make these activities a part of your own lifestyle. If, like Dave Navarro, your passion is to reach out to Latin populations in Pacoima, then spend your Saturday mornings in the parks in Pacoima. Sit down with people on the benches there and ask the Lord to lead you to the believers, or to those who are open to him. Find out who the Christians are and challenge them with your vision as you sit together and look out over the fields white with harvest.

Determine Essential Roles

How many team members will you need to build your initial team? This depends on the size and complexity of your task, and the roles that you have identified that need to be filled. Your initial team will usually be between three and ten individuals.

Think through what kinds of people you will need. Here's a list to get you started.

- Recruiter/Mobilizer
- Organizer
- Evangelist
- Administrator (financial if needed)
- Technically skilled people
- Workers

As you get to know people, generate a list of potential team members, but do not yet make any firm invitations. Your list, when complete, must be at least twice, and preferably three times, the size of your projected initial team before you can proceed to the next step.

Brainstorm Names

Sit down with your list and prayerfully brainstorm for the names of other individuals who might be potential team members. Who has completed tasks in your church and demonstrated abilities that your team will need to complete its mission? Don't simply jot down the names of friends, but think in terms of skill sets and demonstrated leadership abilities.

Don't be afraid to include on your list the names of those who are already actively involved in other ministries, particularly if they are demonstrating success in leadership and service in those ministries. It never hurts to consider everyone. As a matter of fact, it will usually help your ministry in the long run, even if the people you have asked indicate that they are unable or uninterested. It gives you an early opportunity to share your vision with those individuals, to gain their valuable support and their ownership of your ministry even if they don't end up being a part of your initial team. It also encourages them by affirming their character, gifts, and abilities.

Your list of names should now be at least three times the size of the needed team.

Go Public

The next step will be to present a public-information meeting during which you will share your vision (the need and how it can be filled), as well as your passion and plan for meeting that need. Thorough advance preparation for this informational meeting will be as important a part of the recruitment process as the meeting itself. Here are the steps to prepare for the meeting:

1. Pray for wisdom and creativity on how best to present your meeting. Also pray that God will move the right individuals to attend your meeting.
2. Next, plan the time and place. Find a time when your target audience is most likely to be available. Consult the key people on your list of potential team members. Reserve a room or a place and the time on your church calendar.
3. Start your advance publicity, which should go into effect between two and three weeks prior to your meeting.

   Write an article for your church newsletter and submit it to the editor, along with a personal invitation to attend and find out more. (If the newsletter uses photographs, submit any good photographs or artwork that will demonstrate or illustrate the need and the way in which you will be attempting to meet it.)

   Write an announcement for your weekend worship bulletin, or whatever printed forum your church uses, in addition to or in place of a newsletter. When writing articles or newsletters, be sure to make telephone or personal contact with the editor to ensure that he or she understands the nature of your announcement.

   Write a note and personally ask whoever is in charge of making public announcements to the congregation, during worship services or other church meetings, to make the announcement.

   Compose a flyer. It does not have to be a fancy typeset job; creativity is more important. Design one that can be easily and inexpensively photocopied. If you can't type or print neatly, find someone in the church who will help you. With recent innovations in personal computing, there is now someone in nearly every church equipped with a personal computer and laser printer or other high quality printer who can produce flyers with a professional typeset look. Frequently these individuals have entire libraries of electronic clip art, or else they can scan your black and white illustrations for inclusion.

   Distribute your flyers. Include them in the worship bulletin or set them in key places where information is disseminated in your church; but don't leave it at that. The most effective way is to recruit several people who will hand them, with a smile, to people as they are leaving your worship service. This puts a friendly face behind your announcement and also effectively invites the people who are handing out your flyers to join your team.

4. Issue special "engraved invitations" to the individuals on your list of possible team members. When issuing an invitation, or making any other approach to people in which a response on their part is important, always use the following three-step process: (1) Call. Do not ask for a decision, but simply let people know an invitation is coming in the mail and ask them to look for it. (2) Write. Send your invitation by mail, including all essential details. Do not ask them to R.S.V.P., but indicate that you will call for their response. (3) Call again. Ask for their response.

5. Plan your meeting. Remember the basic principle of compassion: Appeal to people's hearts as well as their minds. People need to see the need before they will be moved with compassion. And they need to see how they can help meet the need. Remember that people respond to communication in a combination of the following three ways:

   Audio. Some people are most impacted by discussion or oral presentation. They won't even look at a printed proposal. They want to hear about it, in order to best process it.

   Visual. Others want to see a concept graphically represented. Videos, photographs, multimedia presentations that move the heart as well as feed the mind are always very useful.

   Printed. Some people need something printed to take home, which they can later study, so something will be absorbed. Prepare a simple ministry proposal containing your summary of the need and how it can be met. (For more guidance on preparing a ministry proposal, refer to the material in the next two chapters, which goes into much more detail on the subject.)

6. The day before the meeting, call everyone who has responded positively, just to remind them. A simple and cheery message on their answering machine, if that is all you get, should be sufficient.

With plenty of advance work, your meeting should be a success. Now you can focus your energies on praying for the people that God will draw to your informational meeting.

Use your informational meeting not only to share information about your vision, but also to get to know those who have attended. Share with them that you are not issuing open invitations to be a part of the ministry, but you are instead seeking the Lord to build a ministry team, and you want to hear their heart as well. This will prepare your team for the next step.

Selecting Your Initial Team

This is a unique aspect of the process that we are asking you to consider. Almost always, when volunteer ministries are formed, we say to the Lord, "We'll take anyone you bring us." Whoever shows an interest, whoever shows up, they're automatically a part of the team. At that point we quit searching for new team members, and start using whomever we've got to try to work our plan.

This is substantially different than the process we are proposing, which is much more intentional and more selective. It recognizes that there may be times when someone expresses an interest in being a part of your ministry team, but you will instead thank them and say, "I appreciate your interest, but I do not at this time feel that God is leading you to be a part of the core team."

This may be a bit startling, but it is the process that Christ used in selecting the Twelve. As Christ walked through Galilee, he generated a large group of disciples. Some time after Christ had selected the Twelve, John 6:66 reveals that many of his disciples turned away and no longer followed him, but the Twelve remained. In Acts 1, before the descent of the Holy Spirit, 120 disciples of Christ were gathered in one place.

Christ's task was to select, from among this larger group, a smaller group of men who would be his basic leadership team. Not that he abandoned the larger group of disciples; at one point seventy-two of them were sent out, two by two, to do ministry. But Christ carefully focused his leadership team on twelve men, whom he would work directly with, one-on-one.

What did that focusing process look like? For Christ, it was an intense prayer session, one that lasted all night long: "One of those days Jesus went out to a mountainside to pray, and spent the night praying to God. When morning came, he called his disciples to him and chose twelve of them, whom he also designated apostles" (Luke 6:12–13).

Christ's selection of the disciples was done in an isolated setting. The choice was an important one, and the focus of much intense thought and prayer. Below, in the valley, were the crowds waiting to be ministered to. Too often we do our team preparation "on the fly," in the midst of our busy schedules and busy lives. But to Christ, this was an important issue, one that warranted "stepping away" for a time from the demands of the ministry.

Understanding Team Roles

Karen Johnson was the founder of the Conejo Valley Crisis Pregnancy Center in Thousand Oaks, California. God gave her the vision and the passion for this ministry; she shared her vision and brought together the original team, but then she realized she was not the right person to launch this new ministry. The job demanded a person who had more catalytic skills and a more aggressive style. The Lord had other people in mind for getting it started—their names were Julie Kaiser and Teri Reisser.

Just because God gives you the vision for a ministry does not necessarily mean you ought to lead that ministry. Your role may simply be to articulate that vision and build a team. Or, you may be the person to lead a ministry, after someone else conceived a vision for it. Moreover, different types of leaders may be necessary for a ministry in different stages of life. A new ministry, like the Thousand Oaks center, needs a pioneering person, a catalytic person, one who can create and articulate vision. But sometimes these types of people aren't equipped for actually setting the wheels of their ideas into motion, or for managing the day-to-day activities of such a ministry once it has been established. They grow bored or burn out easily.

Ultimately, Karen's passion found new expression as she developed her leadership skills. Although she was not the one to launch it initially, she is now leading this ministry as its director.

The fact is, God has created us differently. We each have different working styles, different environments in which we are comfortable. Sometimes our abilities change, depending on the need at hand. But for each of us, there is an ideal working environment, and we are most effective when we figure out what that is and put ourselves in it.

But how do you do that? How do you understand what type of a person you are?

The best teacher is experience, and the best way to understand your working style is by looking at your past. Each of us has a history of jobs and experiences, some good, some not so good. Think back through your past experiences, to a time when you were happiest and most effective. What were you doing? (And don't say, "Lounging on the beach at Maui"—that doesn't count.)

What God has created us to do is sometimes best understood by looking at what we have done, or at least what we have done indicates who we are. Look at the history of your working relationship with others. Have you always responded to the lead of others, or have you been an initiator? Do you prefer inventing new environments, new structures in which people can work—or would you rather take a structure that someone else has created and make it work? Do most of your projects involve the assistance of other people, or would you rather work with theoretical systems in such a way that you are not burdened with the confusing dynamics of interpersonal interactions? We are exaggerating a bit to make our point, but hopefully you see what it is.

There have been a number of efforts to quantify and categorize human working styles, and to understand how they interact together. One helpful resource in this process is the book *Finding a Job You Can Love.*[1]

Obviously, any successful ministry needs a variety of people. It needs someone to create and express the vision, someone to take the vision and figure out how to make it into a process that works, and someone to take the vision and the process and work it. The problem that you will be confronted with, in making your team selections, is this: How do you understand which people are what type? And how do you assign them to a role that will fit their working style?

Assessment

In assessing potential team members, there are four areas in which you will need to exercise discernment:

- Passion
- Personality
- Giftedness
- Skills

The assessment is carried out by conducting an interview in which you ask general questions designed to determine how a person's working style has been demonstrated through his or her work experiences. In other words, what is it about a person's history (not hopes and ambitions) that demonstrates how he or she would function on your team?

These are the sorts of questions that must therefore be asked in order to come to an understanding of a person's experience and what it says about the person's passion, personality, giftedness, and skills:

- Tell me about an experience you had when you were a child, some project that you did that made you feel happy and fulfilled. What was your role in this project? What happened?
- Do the same for an experience you had in junior high or high school, and one in college or young adulthood (if applicable).
- Now think of a time when you felt miserable, unproductive, and unfulfilled. What was your role then? Why did you feel that way?

Realize that in any interview, the respondent is trying to please you, to give you the answers you want to hear. The person will need to be assured that the interview is for his or her benefit, so that you will be able to understand what role he or she has been created to do, and so that you will not give that person a role where he or she will be unhappy. All of the respondents must understand that your assessment of them is not a pass-fail device, but is designed only to help you understand where they would be happiest on the team.

Understanding Team Life Cycles

One of the strengths of the church-growth movement is the way that it has come to understand local churches, not only as organizations, but as *organisms*. An organism is a living thing, and one characteristic of living things is that they go through life cycles—they are conceived, they are nurtured in an embryonic form, they are born, they grow, they plateau, they reproduce, and at some point they most likely grow frail and die.

It may be helpful to think of our ministry organizations, as well, being organisms that are characterized by phases of life. We must realize, too, that different types of leadership may be required in the different phases of life. The catalytic person may be exceptionally suited for conceiving a ministry, and possibly nurturing it through the embryonic phase, maybe even birthing it. However, the childhood phase of an organism will require a different type of leadership.

At this or some other point the catalytic person may either need to transfer leadership to an organizer type and step aside, or else adapt his or her own role to that of an organizer.

Part of the strategic planning process is recognizing that these phase changes are coming, and preparing for them—by training the necessary leadership to fulfill its anticipated roles. The catalyst must immediately recognize that he or she may not be suitable to organize and operate his or her ministry for the long haul. Therefore, he or she must intentionally focus on raising up, motivating, and training organizational and operative leadership for the future if that ministry is to continue growing.

The Challenge of Delegation

A challenge that seriously diminishes the success of most lay-led ministry endeavors is the tendency to accumulate and centralize control in the hands of whoever has the strongest ownership of the vision of the organization—usually its founder. Organization founders feel so deeply about their vision for ministry that they fear what would happen if they were to release control over the process to others. The slogan of these people is, "If you want something done right, you have to do it yourself"—and that's precisely what happens; they end up doing everything themselves. When they eventually and finally burn out or die, the vision dies with them.

Problems frequently arise when a catalyst's vision for ministry is insufficiently resourced with organizers and workers to conduct that ministry. Effective delegation assigns every task that can possibly be assigned to a subordinate, then builds in the follow-up instrument that ensures that the task will be completed according to a set schedule.[2]

Training for Focused Service

Serving God and doing ministry, Paul recognized, was not simply a matter of "walking in the path" of the good works that God has prepared for us. It is also hard work:

> Everyone who competes in the games goes into strict training. They do it to get a crown that will not last; but we do it to get a crown that will last forever. Therefore I do not run like a man running aimlessly; I do not fight like a man beating the air. No, I beat my body and make it my slave so that after I

have preached to others, I myself will not be disqualified for the prize.

1 Corinthians 9:25–27

Paul's metaphor here is sure to offend all of us who are so-called couch potatoes at heart. "He 'beat his body'? Heavens no, Lord! Being a Christian is supposed to be *fun* . . . and *that* doesn't sound like fun at all."

No, the truth is that if we are to truly serve others, we must work at it. We must "go into strict training." Now, this doesn't necessarily mean a seminary education. But "training" does imply that we are to do far more than to simply jump into a ministry role and expect God to start dropping fruit into our laps. No, there will be preparation.

How do you focus your training? The first step is knowing what you're in training for. This argues very strongly for an intensive effort in coming to understand how God has created you, how he has gifted you, and how you are to use those gifts. You must discover precisely what it is he desires you to do, and how you are to go about it. Armed with this knowledge, we may then proceed to plan our training path.

The process of training is one of your most important challenges. What is the most effective way to train team members? How do you impart skills as well as deal with the broader issues of discipling? Here are seven principles to bear in mind.

- Mentoring
- Giving freedom to fail
- Storytelling
- Modeling
- Empowering
- Releasing
- Celebrating landmarks

Mentoring. Every Timothy needs a Paul, and every Paul should have a Timothy. Successful teams are those in which the loss of any one individual is minimized by the fact that that individual has been training a second individual to fill his or her shoes in just such an eventuality. Each team member should understand that it is his or her responsibility to be both apprentice and mentor; every person should be actively involved in two training relationships simultaneously.[3]

Giving freedom to fail. Disciples learn by trial and error—we desire to avoid failure, setting a standard of personal holiness; but we must not be afraid of failure. Peter's denial of Christ and subsequent restoration helps us realize that Christ anticipates failure and looks beyond it. The key is our attitude—humility recognizes that failure can and will come at any time. Taking sober control of our thoughts and disciplining our minds keeps us alert against the possibility of failure. Failures can be mistakes or sins, or both: If we make a mistake, we recognize it quickly and correct the perceptions, conditions, and actions that led to the mistake. If we sin, we repent quickly and apply 1 John 1:9 (confession to God) and James 5:16 (transparency before our fellow believers and confession to them), not forgetting the role of restorative prayer.

Storytelling. Clearly an important role of the mentor is to be a teacher. Christ spent much of his time teaching. Sometimes he would be teaching to the crowds, but his parable was aimed at his disciples who were listening in from the sides. Afterward he would debrief with them, and give them the keys for understanding the parable if they needed them. Christ always sought to link spiritual truths with real-life metaphors the people would understand, whether the links were farming or ranching or fishing or whatever. This means we must understand and take into serious account the lifestyles of those we mentor. If we are mentoring an autoworker, perhaps we want to teach about discipling in the language of quality control.

Modeling. Christ modeled appropriate behaviors before his disciples. He was on the lookout for opportunities to model key values. He would model an action, then take them aside and explain its significance, exhorting them to do likewise. A good modeling scheme is: (1) Both of us go out together on an activity. You watch while I do. Then we debrief. (2) We do the activity together, then debrief. (3) I watch while you do, then evaluate. (4) You go out by yourself and do the activity. When you come back we discuss.

Empowering. Christ sent out his disciples to do ministry, expressing his confidence in them. The pastor should equip others, not just do the work himself or herself. Likewise, the goal of a ministry leader/trainer/mentor should be to equip the disciple to do the ministry, and to supervise as it is done—not to do it himself or herself.

There is a marked difference between churches and pastors who give people permission or license to do ministry, and those who do not. John Jubile, whose compassion ministry takes him and his brother Jim south of the border to work on various construction projects, recalls, "That's one of the things that really impressed me about Community Baptist Church of Alta Loma. When we shared our vision for ministry, the church said, 'Go for it.' They gave us the permission and the encouragement."

Releasing. After modeling appropriate behaviors, Christ frequently threw his disciples into the water to sink or swim. He gave basic instruction, then sent the seventy-two out to heal and cast out demons. But he always debriefed with them afterward. He took advantage either of their frustration (when they were at a point of need) or their exultation (when they were excited and he really had their attention) to drive home his points. What does this mean for our training? It must be hands-on, on-the-job. Because they learn by doing ministry, we don't make it too easy for people, or rescue them from potential learning experiences. We work with them to help them understand the goal, and then model or teach some possible methods—letting them work out their own methodology and discover their own path to achieving the goal.

Celebrating landmarks (evaluating progress, designing threshold events). A disciple will have been graduated to a certain level after proving that he can do thus and thus effectively on his own. As leaders we must celebrate and affirm that graduation.

Your Team's Relationship to the Church

The term *sodality* comes from the Roman Catholic Church, where it is used to refer to "a lay society for devotional or charitable activity." Webster defines sodality simply as a "fellowship, association, or brotherhood." Unlike *modality,* the word *sodality* has no root.

Modality, on the other hand, is defined by Webster as "the state or quality of being modal." And *modal* is defined as "of or indicating a mode or mood." Clearly that does not help us much.

Church-growth experts use the terms to anthropologically distinguish groups of people by their focus. Modalities are member-focused. In other words, the group exists primarily for the sake of the group—to build up its members, to accomplish something in their lives. It exists to meet its members' needs.

A good analogy of a modality may be a city or a town. The people who live in a given area form a city or a town in order to meet certain needs that they have—for protection (police and fire), for civic services such as water, power, waste disposal, and for social needs. There isn't much in the way of prerequisite for being a member of a city. You simply have to live within the boundary and cooperate to a certain extent with everyone else to live together harmoniously.

A sodality, on the other hand, is a team that is focused on task. A business venture may be a good analogy. People can come and go; their membership on the team is defined by their ability to contribute toward completion of the team's task.

An ongoing debate in recent times has been over how you classify the church, at least in terms of modality-sodality models. The four easily identified functions of the church can be expressed by the following four metaphors: family, school, hospital, army. The first three are obviously all modalic functions. Families exist to service their members. So do schools and hospitals, in different ways. Armies, on the other hand, exist to advance an external purpose—to move out and achieve certain goals. Individual soldiers are important to the function of an army, but they are not the focus of it. The focus is on completing the army's task, whether defense or offense. Individual soldiers can get killed in the line of duty, and the army hasn't failed its task. If members of a family, school, or hospital are killed in the line of duty, however, chances are that institution has failed in its task, which is generally to keep those members alive and healthy.

Now, can individual local churches have a sodalic expression? Certainly. Lawndale Community Church is a fine example. It is definitely a modality, ministering to the needs of its members. But it attempts some sodalic functions. It has a function of moving out into the community and accomplishing certain things, like social justice. It includes some army functions along with the family, school, and hospital.

However, churches as modalic entities experience certain difficulties in functioning as sodalic entities. Some difficulties are inherent in the model, and others are a result of expectations of our society or culture. Let's look at an example of both.

Example One: Church A employs its volunteers in the task of feeding the hungry in its community. But in this particular community, the need is tremendous. In order to function effectively and meet the need, those volunteers must operate on the level of professionals.

Date June 3 19___

M _____

No. _____

Reg. No.	Clerk	ACCOUNT FORWARD		
1	Cork			9 9 9
2				9 9
3			9	9 00
4		7 4		7 4
5				9 74
6				
7				
8				
9				
10				
11				
12				
13				
14				
15		22		

Your Account Stated to Date—If Error Is Found Return at Once.

This means the pastor has become the manager of a staff of professional social-service workers. He has become confronted with the arduous task of selecting one "applicant" for a management position over another. And what happens when he feels the need to "fire" a church member, a volunteer in a key leadership position, because of incompetence?

Example Two: Church B establishes a ministry that seeks to diminish the role of pornographers in the community. Some of the elderly women in the ministry bake cookies and then take them to the front of the local nude-dancing establishment where they set up tables and offer cookies and milk to the men who are trying to enter discreetly. They have discovered that many of the men turn ashamedly away when they discover the presence of the women.

All seems well until the church's lawyer advises the church administrator that there is a high degree of risk in the ladies' behavior. It seems that other establishments have sued such groups in court for interfering in their stock and trade. As well, the lawyer fears a certain degree of physical risk to the ministry's volunteers, and the liability that incurs. The pastor doesn't want to shut down an effective ministry, however. What does he do?

For different reasons, both pastors are struggling with the implications of sodalic ministry arising within a context that is essentially modalic. It was reasons very similar to these (in addition to the conviction on the part of many lay leaders that the church as a modality was too cautious and insufficiently proactive in fulfilling its role of meeting human needs outside the four walls of the church) that spurred the creation of sodalic ministries throughout history.

When a Lay Leader Should Stay Modalic

Many ministries will operate very well within the modalic parameters of the average local church. The questions to ask are:

- What are the values of the church? How well does the proposed ministry synchronize with those values? How excited is the pastoral staff about this ministry being done under the name of this local church?

- What are the staff requirements of this ministry? How task oriented must the volunteers be? Is there the possibility of having to fire a team member for failure to perform the task?
- What is the risk presented to the church by this ministry? Is it likely to get too big for the church or have undue influence on the church's identity? Is there the possibility of lawsuit or other danger to the church brought on by the ministry?
- What is the potential for leadership conflict? Is there any danger in the ministry leader's being fully subordinate to the pastoral authority of the church?
- What about resources? Will the ministry either require or consume an inordinate level of resources, compared to other ministries operating within the church?
- Would effectiveness of scope be greater without structural limitations of the modality?

When a Lay Leader Must Go Sodalic

Basically, a ministry should consider going sodalic when the answer to many of the above questions becomes yes. If a ministry gets too big for a church (in terms of its identity or its requirement for resources), when it becomes too risky, when the importance of team members who are focused on the task becomes too great, then a ministry should consider officially being more organizationally autonomous, and operating on its own either as a voluntary association, a business venture, a sole proprietorship, or an independent mission organization.

Interdependence: A Model for Modalic/Sodalic Relationship

Simply because a ministry goes independent does not mean it should be abandoned by the church modal form. The most effective sodalities operate interdependently with modalities. They communicate regularly, and frequently trade volunteers and other personnel back and forth. They provide opportunities to church members for the expression of compassionate ministry, and help those members take their learning experiences back to the local churches. The churches, on the other hand, provide desperately needed volunteers and financial resources to those ministries. Effective ministries operate in close symbiosis with local churches.

One Ministry's Journey from Modality to Sodality to Interdependence

Circle Urban Ministries in Chicago is a good example of a ministry that has made this journey from modality, to sodality, to interdependence. The ministry began as an outreach of a racially mixed church in Chicago. When the church split, the ministry moved into a huge abandoned high school facility and became a fully functional sodality. Eventually, they attracted the attention of another church, whose pastor was in full harmony with the vision of the ministry. The new church even used the ministry facilities for its meeting place. A unique interdependence now exists between the two, wherein each provides both resources and opportunities for the other.

The kingdom of God will never be advanced by modalities and sodalities arguing among themselves or trying to go it alone, denying the historical or biblical legitimacy of either. We need to look for and emulate the many fine examples where the church in local form (modalities) and the church in task-mobile form (sodalities) are living and working side by side in harmonious symbiosis.

The Team Training Process

Most problems that arise in team interaction are the result of conflicts with either the ministry's vision, its core values, or else its mission statement. Since the vision is what draws the team in to begin with, if there is a problem with the vision, it is going to be with the team member's understanding or perception of it.

Your initial team members should go with you through the process of gaining vision, clarifying core values, and establishing a mission statement. Teams that succeed are those where the vision, values, and mission statements are owned by the entire team, rather than by just its leader.

This is a complex and crucial process, but there are some simple tools you can use to make it both easier and more effective. In the next chapter we will look at these tools and how they work together to form a strategic planning process that will put feet on your vision.

Action Idea Checklist

☐ Ask the Lord to raise up workers and effective teams for the harvest.

☐ Assess your most effective role(s) on a team; identify what other kinds of people you need around you.
☐ Recruit a team that shares your vision.
☐ Identify areas for training within your team.
☐ Think through the team's relationship to your church.

Add your own follow-up items below.

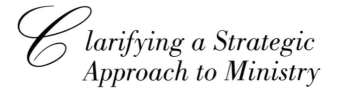

Clarifying a Strategic Approach to Ministry

How Vision Empowers Ministry

What distinguishes people from animals? In what ways are humans created "in the image of God"?

One of these ways is our innate ability to experience vision, that is, to conceptualize in the context of an accurate understanding of the present a future that is brighter, a future in which some problem or other has been solved. Like the servant of Elisha, we have the ability at times to perceive the spiritual reality beyond the physical reality. Such vision is a function of hope and faith. The hope for this potential reality drives the engine of enthusiastic and interdependent action, and visualization also enables human beings to focus the attitudes and actions necessary to bring this future to a reality; so that in a very real sense, vision is self-fulfilling prophecy.

The leader with vision asks himself or herself: *If God has his way, what will the results of this ministry be ten years from now? How will people's needs be met? How will their lives be bettered? In what ways will people be reconciled to God? And what will be the results of faithful service in our own lives?*

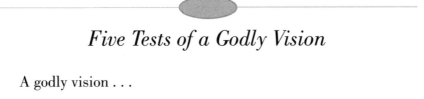

Five Tests of a Godly Vision

A godly vision . . .

- Is right for the times
- Promotes faith rather than fear
- Motivates people to action
- Requires some risk-taking
- Glorifies God, not people

A godly vision is right for the times. Dieter Zander is the pastor of New Song Church in Walnut, California. New Song is the daughter church of Community Baptist Church, which was established with the vision to reach baby boomers. At the time that New Song was established, *baby busters* was barely a term in our vocabulary. Yet Dieter had a vision to reach a group of "twentysomethings" who had needs that he realized were in many ways being ignored by our society.

The vision turned out to be right for the times, catching a group of individuals in flux just as they were graduating from college and establishing their lives. It was right for the young church, which grew rapidly. And it was right for the people: Hundreds of students and other young people have discovered a church that offers a previously unexperienced relevance to their lifestyles.

A godly vision promotes faith rather than fear. A godly vision will stretch. It always expands our borders. The only way to test the resources of God is to attempt the impossible in his name.

This doesn't mean that the saints of God will consider doing his will to be "easy." But God asks us to have courage. We know that courage is not the absence of fear, but rather the presence of faith that is greater than our fear.

A godly vision motivates people to action. It never increases complacency, but always stirs the heart and lifts us to a higher plane. It is never satisfied with merely feeling, but it always seeks a powerful manifestation of sacrificial love.

A godly vision requires some risk-taking. Charles Swindoll says, "Great accomplishments are often attempted but only occasionally reached. What is interesting (and encouraging) is that those who reach them are usually those who missed many times before. Failures, you see, are only temporary tests to prepare us for the permanent triumphs."[1] While we attempt great things for God, we maintain the freedom to fail. Failure is only permanent when we give up and refuse to try again.

A godly vision glorifies God, not people. In this society we have seen the results of the visions of many. Perhaps they started well, but at some point they became empires built to lift up self. What is needed, instead of empire builders, are kingdom builders—those who would be willing to attempt great things for the sake of the kingdom, while maintaining the true ability to die to self, to remove oneself from the picture (or at least to move into the background) if that is what is called for in the quest to glorify the name of God.

We are living in days when, as Christians, we are called to go the second mile. Ordinary Christianity is not enough; more is demanded. We desperately need to experience a greater reality of the presence and power of God in our lives. We desperately need to be touched by godly vision.

The Vision Tree

The Vision Tree, developed by Bob Logan and Steve Ogne, helps us visualize the relationship among principles, values, our mission statement, ministry areas designed for the accomplishment of our purpose, specific goals and objectives, and the results of our ministry (the accomplishment of those goals and objectives). It is a holistic perception of the role each of these things play in contribution to vision.

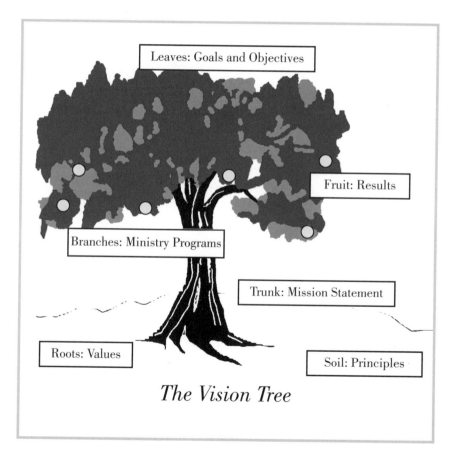

Leaves: Goals and Objectives

Fruit: Results

Branches: Ministry Programs

Trunk: Mission Statement

Roots: Values

Soil: Principles

The Vision Tree

The Soil: Timeless Principles

In seeking to get to the core of how our behavior and relationships can contribute to our success or failure, Stephen Covey wrote a book whose thesis was that our lives should be centered on what he called the fundamental, natural, immutable principles that govern the universe of human relationships.

> Principles are the guidelines for human conduct that are proven to have enduring, permanent value. They're fundamental. They're essentially inarguable because they are self-evident. One way to quickly grasp the self-evident nature of principles is to simply consider the absurdity of attempting to live an effective life based on their opposites. I doubt that anyone would seriously consider unfairness, deceit, baseness, uselessness, mediocrity, or degeneration to be a solid foundation for lasting happiness and success.[2]

You and I as Christians know where these principles come from. They are not simply "innate, natural laws" intelligent people have discovered that better their lives. Rather, they are principles that have been revealed by a holy God, whom we must model our lives after in order to truly "succeed." These principles are right for us because they are characteristics of him.

As Christians we recognize that to be so-called successful as God's children, we must base our value system on these revealed biblical principles. The principles can therefore be likened to the soil from which our values draw their nourishment; they are the environment in which these values are formed.

Psalm 1:3 says of the man who meditates on God's Word, "He is like a tree planted by streams of water, which yields its fruit in season and whose leaf does not wither. Whatever he does prospers." Christ indicated that rivers or streams of water are a metaphor for the Holy Spirit (John 7:38–39, Ps. 42:1, Rev. 22:1–2). If our "tree" is planted near streams of living water—that is, if the Holy Spirit directs and indwells our ministry efforts—we are given assurance that not only will we bear fruit, but we will bear it monthly—twelve times as much as an ordinary tree would!

Roots: Core Values

Values are the often unwritten assumptions that guide our actions. Our values as Christians flow from our view of who God is, and they determine both our behavior and our attitudes. If God is truly loving, kind, and compassionate, then love, kindness, and compassion become our core values. The way that we minister must therefore exhibit love, compassion, and kindness. Our attitudes flow from values that take their cue from the principles established by the model of Christ, and these attitudes result in godly actions:

> Your attitude should be the same as that of Christ Jesus: Who, being in very nature God, did not consider equality with God something to be grasped, but made himself nothing, taking the very nature of a servant, being made in human likeness. And being found in appearance as a man, he humbled himself and became obedient to death—even death on a cross!
>
> Therefore, my dear friends, as you have always obeyed—not only in my presence, but now much more in my absence—continue to work out your salvation with fear and trembling, for it is God who works in you to will and to act according to his good purpose.
>
> *Philippians 2:5–8, 12–13*

Our values demonstrate our convictions, or our heartfelt beliefs, and they also determine our priorities. For instance, one of our values may be that ministry must affirm the intrinsic dignity of people. That value will help us prioritize our ministry of feeding the hungry: We will choose to feed them in ways that affirm their dignity. If different ways of feeding them are at our disposal, we will place a higher priority on those methods that affirm dignity over those methods that do not.

Remember, our values are not a doctrinal statement; rather, they are convictions based on biblical principles that we hold dear and that will determine how we will operate our ministry. For example, our doctrinal statement may say that the ministry believes that all the gifts stated in the Bible are available to the body of Christ today. The biblical principle is that God gives gifts to his children to be used in ministry. The value derived from this principle says that we will celebrate the unique giftedness of people by encouraging them to discover and use their spiritual gifts. This value will affect our attitudes and behavior: We will exhibit a positive attitude when we see our team members using their particular gifts to minister to the needy, even if this means we must accept some flexibility in the manner in which that ministry is done. Our behavior will demonstrate this value in that we will affirm and seek to further empower the person who is using his or her unique spiritual gifts in ministry.

Values provide the foundation for formulating goals and setting the direction of our ministry. The first step in this process is to sit down and diagram the various principles that we believe are foundational to our ministry effort, and then the values that they give rise to. The example on the next page offers some sample core values that might be shared by urban ministries to the poor. For the sake of example, we have limited it to just a small handful of values; your chart will be much more comprehensive.

After you have brainstormed all your values, the second step is to arrange them into similar groups, and then to boil them down, if you can—that is, to cluster like values together. Next, prioritize your values. Select between five and ten of the most important values.

What you should now have is a prioritized list of your core values, your five to ten key statements that reflect the distinctives of your ministry—that is, *how* you will perform your ministry. Next take each core value and write next to it associated relevant *behavior(s)*. (See the sample core-values chart on page 116.)

TWO TYPES OF VALUES. There are two broad categories of values that have application to what we are considering here: *team values,* which deal with the manner in which we relate to one another; and *ministry values,* which deal with the manner in which we will work our ministry plan and seek to meet people's needs. However, the same charts could be used to diagram team values.

WHY ARE VALUES IMPORTANT? Conflict in ministry endeavors frequently arises from differing expectations. This happens when values are not articulated at the beginning of the strategic planning process. As an example, take the ministry of InnerCHANGE, led by John Hayes in Long Beach, California. InnerCHANGE holds the value that ministry must be personal, that is, you go out on the streets and get to know people, and in getting to know them you see how you can help them as individuals. This value leads to the belief that something that helps one person is not necessarily going to help another.

Core Values Chart for: *Sample Urban Ministry*

Principles ———————➤ Resulting Values

Principles	Resulting Values
The Gospel is expressed through both our words and our works (John 10:37–38; 14:10–11; Rom. 15:18–19; James 1:27).	**Evangelism** We will express the Good News through both word and works, without placing one above another.
Christ left the wealth and power of his heavenly position to identify incarnationally with the world's needy (John 1:14; Phil. 2:6–8).	**Identification** We will identify incarnationally with the needy, living where they live and being where they are.
Christ developed personal relationships that gave insight into people's needs. He met those needs one at a time (Luke 14:12–14; 19:1–10).	**Relationships** We will minister God's reconciliation primarily through personal relationships.
We are exhorted to wage war against spiritual forces in high places, using spiritual weapons (Eph. 6:12; 2 Cor. 10:3–5).	**Spiritual Warfare** We will commit to spiritual warfare on behalf of our neighbors, freeing them from their captivity.
God shows us mercy and commands that as an act of devotion we exercise justice to the poor (Matt. 23:23; Isa. 58:6–9; Mic. 6:8).	**Justice and Mercy** We will commit to promote justice and mercy in the same manner we pursue personal growth and piety.
Our commitment to Christ is demonstrated in oneness of heart and loving one another (John 13:35; 17:22–23; Eccles. 4:9–12).	**Community** We will model healthy kingdom communities among our staff and volunteers.
God goes ahead of us, in the spiritual realm, to guide us and guard our paths (Exod. 23:20; John 16:13–15; Acts 16:6–10).	**God's Sovereignty** We will seek God's guidance to discover how he has gone before us to prepare the poor for the Gospel.

Our gratitude goes to InnerCHANGE ministry (Long Beach, Calif.), from whom these sample core values were adapted. Blank forms for your use can be found in appendix C.

Core Values Chart for: *Sample Urban Ministry*

Core Values	→	Resulting Behaviors

Evangelism
We will express the Good News through both word and works, without placing one above another.

As we meet needs we will exercise every opportunity to communicate that God's grace provides the ultimate solution to our problems.

Identification
We will identify incarnationally with the needy, living where they live and being where they are.

All volunteers must live in the same community as our target group, and seek to invest our time in the people we minister to.

Relationships
We will minister God's reconciliation primarily through personal relationships.

We will seek to meet needs one person at a time, getting to know that person and coming to understand how we can truly help him.

Spiritual Warfare
We will commit to spiritual warfare on behalf of our neighbors, freeing them from their captivity.

As a staff we will intercede daily on behalf of the people to whom we are ministering. We will seek in prayer the key to understand them.

Justice and Mercy
We will commit to promote justice and mercy in the same manner we pursue personal growth and piety.

We will act as advocates for the people to whom we minister, speaking out boldly on their behalf against that which oppresses them.

Community
We will model healthy kingdom communities among our staff and volunteers.

As staff we will exercise body life and be actively involved in the local church, as we will seek to involve those to whom we minister.

God's Sovereignty
We will seek God's guidance to discover how he has gone before us to prepare the poor for the Gospel.

We will be flexible in our methodologies of ministry, seeking to meet needs in the way we discern God's direction through daily prayer.

However, there are organizations that take a more programmatic approach to helping impoverished people, and do not hold the value that ministry is personal in as high a priority. They might conduct their compassionate ministry, instead, by raising large sums of money to purchase crates of food and clothing to send to help impoverished people in some other country. This lack of a personal value is neither good nor bad; it's just a different way of doing ministry.

But if someone came to InnerCHANGE and expected to do ministry that way in Long Beach, there would be conflicts between that person and the others on staff, because InnerCHANGE holds the value that the ministry they do should be personal, not programmatic. If such a value is stated up front as team members are recruited and trained, it is less likely there will be undue expectations about doing ministry in any other way than individually and personally; if a person starts to tell team members he wants to raise money to send crates of food to Bosnia, the others will tell him, "Well, that sounds like a good idea for some other ministry, but perhaps you're forgetting our value that ministry must be personal." Many conflicts can therefore be avoided before they start because of the core values that are already in place and written down for all to see—values with which ministry team members must agree before they are hired on.

HOW DO YOU DETERMINE VALUES? Your existing actions and emotions are both clues as to the values that you hold dear. In other words, you can sit down and extrapolate your values by the way you feel about issues, and act out your commitment to principles by the way you act to meet needs.

Values Questions

- If the church was really being the church, what types of things would it be doing?
- What types of things make you angry?
- What do you get passionate about?
- How do you invest your time and money?
- What's your biggest criticism of the church?
- What would you like your ministry to be known for?

The preceding set of questions probes how you feel and how you act; the answers to these questions may help you determine some of your values.

Be sure to compare your answers to these questions against biblical principles. Your own priorities and feelings must be in alignment with those modeled by Christ before you can extrapolate your core values from them.

STEPS TO DETERMINING CORE VALUES. In summary:

1. Brainstorm a list of potential core values. Make sure each value is easily translated into actions.
2. Group similar values together and combine.
3. Highlight the ones that are most important. Prioritize.
4. Select four to seven core values.
5. Check for completeness. Do all essential activities in your ministry flow logically from the core values?
6. Describe the specific behaviors that will demonstrate each core value in action. Ask questions like: "How is this going to be lived out?" By linking core values to specific behaviors, you will help members understand the implications of their ministry methods, and clarify their expectations.

For example, a key core value in our hypothetical chart on page 116 deals with evangelism. After establishing this value, our urban ministry team would ask, "How are we going to build evangelism into the activities of this ministry?" The answers will provide a list of specific behaviors.

Our use of this particular example is intentional. We hope and pray that your Christian compassion ministry will see the mandate for spiritual reconciliation as your first and foremost core value. Regardless of the type of ministry established, one of your highest core values ought to be evangelism. This will affirm the symbiotic relationship between the Great Commandment and the Great Commission, which must be recognized and celebrated by all compassionate outreach ministries.

Trunk: Mission Statement

The next step is to write a clear mission statement that expresses your objective and incorporates your core values. Your mission statement should answer these three questions:

- Whom do you seek to minister to (your target group)?
- What specific needs of this target group are you seeking to meet?
- How will you seek to meet these needs?

As you are writing your mission statement, be sure not to confuse *vision* with *mission.* Remember that *vision* paints a picture of a specific future, in the context of an accurate understanding of the present. *Mission,* on the other hand, defines and details your intended strategy to achieve this vision.

SEVEN STEPS TO DEVELOPING A CLEAR MISSION STATEMENT

1. Complete the Principles • Values • Behaviors chart, depicted earlier in this chapter (a blank copy that you can reproduce is included in appendix C). Ensure that there is a biblical foundation for each principle, that each principle has an application expressed in a core value, and that there is a definable attitude or activity associated with each core value.
2. Identify key words and phrases from your principles and values that describe *why* your ministry exists.
3. Compose a simple statement, as concisely as you can, combining the key phrases from your core values.
4. Compose a second brief and very simple statement based on your answer to the question: What is this ministry here for?
5. Now, mold the two into one logically flowing statement that combines the above elements.
6. Evaluate this mission statement by asking these questions:

   - Does it identify your ministry focus group?
   - Does it clarify the needs you seek to meet?
   - Does it identify three to five key ministry areas, describing how the mission will be accomplished?
   - Is it accurate? Enduring? Concise? Memorable? Energizing? (Rewrite if necessary to meet the above criteria.)

7. Create a "theme" embodying your mission statement, in five to ten words.

Peter Drucker articulates three musts for every successful mission statement:

- It should look at *strength* and *performance*. It should elucidate how to do better what you already do well—if it's the right thing to do.
- It should examine both the *needs* and the *opportunities*. Where can you, with limited resources, really make a difference?
- It should portray *what you really believe in*. Says Drucker, "I've never seen anything being done well unless people were committed."[3]

WHAT TO DO WITH YOUR MISSION STATEMENT. Study it, memorize it, and have your team members do the same. Frame it and put it on your wall. Put it in your employee manual. Put it on your letterhead. Celebrate it and use it. Always ask yourself, "How does this activity help us accomplish our mission?" Do anything that it takes, repeating it over and over again, to get its main ideas into the heads of the people who do the ministry in your organization.

Branches: Ministry Areas for the Accomplishment of Purpose

In establishing your mission statement you have already, perhaps, done the lion's share of the work in setting up the direction of your ministry, the three to five main branches or ministry areas where the purpose of your mission will be accomplished. In a moment, we will examine these branches and how they feed into the leaves as we begin to draw a ministry flowchart. But the thing to do at this point is to identify the separate purpose of each area. Each major ministry area must have an achievable and easily stated purpose, or it should be lopped off.

Leaves: Goals and Objectives

Out of each main ministry area, each major branch, will flow specific goals and objectives. For example, if the purpose of the twenty-four-hour suicide hotline is to provide a point of contact with people in crisis, what would be some sample goals for effectively operating this hotline?

- We must have a telephone number—hopefully one that contains a clever acronym so it will be easy to remember.

- We must establish a relationship with an answering service or set up some sort of automated system for delivering the calls to the right people who are on duty at various times.
- We must recruit a sufficient number of hotline counselors.
- We must train those hotline counselors to receive the anticipated calls.
- We must provide them with referral materials and documents that will help us track the callers.
- We must staff the hotline so that principal operators and their back-ups are provided for, twenty-four hours per day, seven days per week.

Many of the above goals, or leaves of the tree, will require a multitude of action steps in order to diagram the path to achievability.

The Fruit: Results of Effective Ministry

The final characteristic of a healthy tree is fruit. There are many reasons that some trees do not bear healthy fruit. Some are not designed to bear fruit; they are merely ornamental—self-perpetuating bureaucracies designed to make those in leadership look or feel good about themselves. Others are not planted in soil that nourishes them adequately; they are not founded on timeless biblical principles; their core values (their roots) are therefore withered, and when the winds blow the whole tree is likely to topple. Others have a diseased trunk, a missing or poorly prepared mission statement that is misunderstood and miscommunicated. The people that make up the organization therefore have no connection with the roots, the core values, and each does whatever seems right in his own eyes, in his own way, with supervision and coordination being impossible. Some trees have weak or damaged branches; there may be some structural weakness in a key program or area of ministry that means fruit that might otherwise be born in that area will not mature. And some have diseased or missing leaves, which represents inadequately defined, misunderstood, unrealistic, unchallenging, or inherently unachievable goals with no accountability, no built-in evaluation process or threshold of success.

However, if there is health in every area of the tree—it is planted deep in nourishing soil, by streams of living water (the blessing of

God and guidance of the Holy Spirit), with vital roots that go deep, a sturdy trunk reaching skyward, strong branches, and healthy green leaves—that tree will bear fruit, and will bear it abundantly. That tree will experience the synergism of effective ministry—its end result (the tasty and delicious fruit) will be greater than the sum of its parts!

A healthy tree is a fruit-bearing tree. An important part of the process of creating a strategic plan is defining what your fruit will be and how you will measure what the quantity and quality of fruit being borne by your tree has to say about its health. Develop your own set of vital signs, or indicators of the state of your ministry's health.

In medicine, vital signs are key indicators of health. They readily provide a "red flag" of serious problems—pulse, respiration, blood pressure, body temperature. What are the vital signs for your ministry?

1. Most ministries have *financial* vital signs, which may be as simple as the figure in your checkbook, or better yet, your balance sheet.
2. There are also *human resources* vital signs, to indicate whether your people are burning out: attendance at meetings, follow-through on commitments, skipping work assignments, and an inability to cover key tasks.
3. And there are *ministry* vital signs, which measure the quality and quantity of the fruit you are producing: Are you achieving your stated ministry goals? Is your ministry developing new and vital relationships with people in your target group? Do they perceive that their needs are being met? Are they being won to Christ and assimilated into the life of a local church?

Define what your vital signs are. What are the indicators in ministry, human resources, finances, or material that measure your effectiveness? What would change if there were a problem? Be sure that you are gathering the necessary information, that the statistics are being monitored by someone and transferred to the right people. As the leader of the ministry, build in the ability to query the system, to check at a glance any specific vital sign. To do this, someone must be given specific responsibility for monitoring key vital signs.

Sometimes ministries collapse seemingly overnight because very simple vital signs were unseen or ignored.

Strategic Tools

The Ministry Flowchart

The purpose of the Ministry Flowchart is to diagram your overall strategy for achieving your mission. Diagramming your programs will help you see the relationships among the areas. Here is how to draw a simple ministry flowchart:

1. Start, on the left side, with your target market. Who are they? Where are they? There may be several distinct groups, or one group that comes to you through several different means. Distinguish these groups or means into separate figures, and place each one on a large Post-it note.
2. List on the right side all ministry programs (branches of your tree) that will serve the needs of the people from the groups indicated on the left.
3. In the middle of the page, diagram how you will reach your target group(s) and carry out your mission. Your drawing should show the logical pathways that ministry should flow through.
4. Think in terms of discipleship. Ask: How do we help people come to faith in Christ and to active participation in a church through our ministry?
5. Identify any missing ministries required to move your target group from one step to the next.

The Post-it Planning Method

The Post-it Planning Method, devised by Bob Logan and Steve Ogne,[4] is a simple yet effective system for doing strategic planning, for breaking down a large project or ministry program (perhaps one of the branches of the Vision Tree) into its component goals and tasks, its working units.

Here's how it works:

1. Lay out a piece of posterboard, newsprint, or whiteboard to serve as a base for your Post-it planning session.

Sample Ministry Flowchart

Ministry: *Church Food Closet*

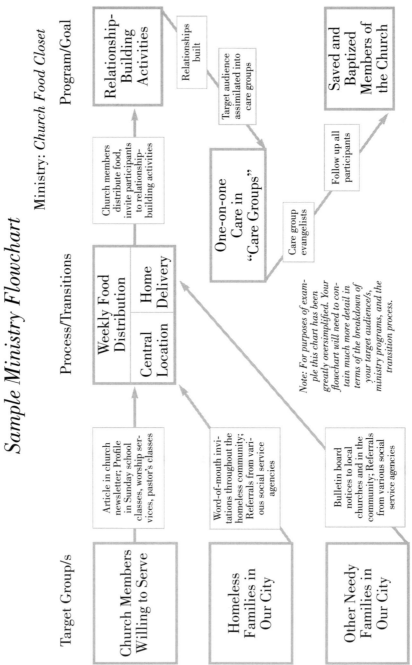

| Target Group/s | Process/Transitions | Program/Goal |

Target Group/s

- Church Members Willing to Serve
- Homeless Families in Our City
- Other Needy Families in Our City

Process/Transitions

Article in church newsletter; Profile in Sunday school classes, worship services, pastor's classes

Word-of-mouth invitations throughout the homeless community; Referrals from various social service agencies

Bulletin board notices to local churches and in the community; Referrals from various social service agencies

Weekly Food Distribution
- Central Location
- Home Delivery

Church members distribute food, invite participants to relationship-building activities

One-on-one Care in "Care Groups"

Target audience assimilated into care groups

Care group evangelists

Follow up all participants

Relationships built

Note: For purposes of example this chart has been greatly oversimplified. Your flowchart will need to contain much more detail in terms of the breakdown of your target audience/s, ministry programs, and the transition process.

Program/Goal

- Relationship-Building Activities
- Saved and Baptized Members of the Church

2. Brainstorm the important milestones required to achieve the goal that is the purpose of the project or ministry program you are planning. Prepare a Post-it for each milestone. Indicate the milestone in the past tense.

3. Arrange the milestones in logical sequence. Ask: Which activities must be completed before others can be begun, or before others can be completed? You will discover that some tasks do not have any connection to each other and can be done simultaneously.

4. Rearrange the milestones in time sequence. Draw a time line across the top of your chart, and put a note at the point at which each Post-it goal must be completed. Maintain the logical relationships between the items, but draw lines spacing out the projects over your time frame as necessary.

5. Identify additional resources needed for accomplishment and note these at the bottom of the chart.

6. Complete your reality checks:

   • Are all steps in their logical sequence?
   • Is the schedule realistic? Examine the diagram carefully. Verify that each aspect of the project is given sufficient lead time for accomplishment. Be realistic about your schedule.
   • Are the personnel or volunteer demands of the project realistic? Does the value of the payoff (successful completion of the goal) warrant the outlay?
   • Are the material or financial demands of the project realistic? Does the value of the payoff (successful completion of the goal) warrant the cost?
   • Do sufficient resources (human, material, and financial) exist for successful completion?
   • Can you identify any gaps where Post-it Notes ought to be (for instance, raising the necessary funds for the project!)?
   • Is each aspect of the project consistent with your core values and statement of mission?

7. Think through the delegation of tasks. Make appropriate assignments and write the name of the responsible person at the bottom of the Post-it Note.

ADVANTAGES OF THE POST-IT PLANNING METHOD

- It helps you develop a comprehensive strategy.
- It can be done individually or in a group setting.
- You don't have to rewrite the tasks.
- You can keep the big picture in front of you, without losing the details.
- It helps you visualize where you're overloaded.
- You can easily change the time sequences by moving the Post-it Notes.
- Using your copy of the planning session, you can easily monitor delegated tasks.

Ready to Go?

Once you've completed your strategic planning efforts, you're ready for a full-scale leap of faith into your project, right? Wrong! The next step is a pilot test of your plan!

Action Idea Checklist

- ☐ Ask God for a clear and specific vision.
- ☐ Articulate your ministry and team values.
- ☐ Focus your mission statement.
- ☐ Diagram your ministry flowchart.
- ☐ Identify your vital signs to measure ministry effectiveness.
- ☐ Use the Post-it planning process to plan your specific steps.
- ☐ Write a clear ministry proposal to communicate your vision and strategy.

Add your own follow-up items below.

6

*C*onducting Compassionate Outreach

Field-Test Your Plans

Why have pilot projects?

It is human nature, when we get excited about an idea, to be overwhelmed with its potential for success. If it weren't such a grand idea, we wouldn't be wasting our time with it, would we? It is hard for us to conceive of the possibility that, flush as we are with the excitement of something new, we might be barking up the wrong tree.

Another tendency of human nature is to rationalize and mix our personal desires with divine mandate. We all can think of a time when we desperately wanted something. We may have prayed briefly, "Lord, please give me this," but we didn't pray thoroughly in a listening mode because we already had ownership of the thing in our hearts and didn't want to let it go. We *really wanted* it!

So we justified our desire with words of faith. "I'm just going to believe God for this thing. After all, he says if my faith is big enough, I can move mountains. I can have whatever I want. And I want this!" Missing in our calculations, of course, is the phrase "according to his will." If we pray according to his will, it will be done for us. But apparently at times we think *our will* is sufficient for both us and God!

Because this is something we really want, and we don't want the humbling experience of being proven wrong, "faith" requires us to look for a maximum investment of resources in our plan. This necessitates our making a supreme effort to sell the idea in order to gain the resources, the backing, of others.

Larry Short relates:

I once had a friend, an outdoorsy type of guy, who was visiting a quaint resort community in nearby mountains when he happened on a large parcel of land that was for sale for about $100,000. Now, back in those days, that was a lot of money; but a strange thing happened to my friend as he stood gazing at that lovely piece of hilly property, breathing deeply the fresh, pine-scented air.

"I had a vision!" he told me excitedly, after demanding urgently that we meet that same day. "God showed me that he wants me to buy that land and put a Christian camp on it, where kids can come to know the Lord in the great outdoors!"

It was a wonderful vision, and my friend was obviously very stirred by it. The problem was, he didn't have the money. My friend had some financial troubles, debts, and I doubt if he had an available $100 in his bank account, let alone that much times one thousand. But the Lord had told him that he wanted him to have the property, and not only that, he wanted him to have it by a certain date, a scant two months away. I was never sure of the reason for this deadline, but if I remember correctly the rapture played into it somewhere.

And what was more, the Lord wanted *me* to invest several thousand dollars into this vision. After all, if only fifty Christian brothers and sisters made this modest investment, God would bless their faith by giving them a part in making this dream come true.

The problem was, I explained to him, I didn't really have $2,000, since I was newly married and just starting out. (Actually, that was a lousy excuse; I still don't have $2,000.) Moreover, when I thought about it, even if I'd had the money, I wouldn't have really wanted to invest it that way.

"Why not?" my friend asked. "Don't you have the faith to believe God can do this?"

"Sure, I believe he could if he wanted to. But will he? Maybe so, maybe not. I don't know. It's your vision—not mine."

That probably was a bit heartless, but it was honest. Albeit, it didn't deter my friend, who continued seeking his fifty investors—probably straining all of his friendships in the process, and doubtless preventing a good many others.

It's probably needless to say, but the two months came and went. Not a single person had contributed a dollar to the purchase, and my friend's dream went unfulfilled. He was a bit bent out of shape about it for awhile, but I think he's forgotten about it now—probably because his wife, in planning the family's leisure travels, has steered him away from that idyllic mountain spot.

The problem this man experienced did not necessarily indicate that the Lord was not behind his vision for a camping ministry. However, God often desires to test the quality of our commitment to a vision for ministry by testing our willingness to humbly accept a smaller initial role. The biblical principle is elaborated in Matthew 25:14–29: The master of a household goes on a long vacation, leaving his three servants with small sums of money—one with one talent, one with two, and one with five. The first hides his talent in the ground; the other two invest and work to double theirs. The "lazy and wicked" servant who has done nothing with his master's resources is severely chastised; but the two servants who worked hard and doubled their master's investment—one returning four talents and the other ten—are praised equally with these words: "Well done, good and faithful servant! You have been faithful with a few things; I will put you in charge of many things. Come and share your master's happiness!"

Before God promises great resources, he requires faithfulness with what he has already given us. This is a very important principle for ministry. We often think, *If we only had thus and thus, boy, could we do great things for God!* But God asks us to prove ourselves faithful in ministry by using what we have been given—our gifts, our skills, our talents, our time, our money—before he will consider adding more resources.

Rather than spending his time trying to raise $100,000 to buy a piece of camp property, the man with a vision for ministering to kids through camping could have sought to join an existing Christian camp. He could have used his car to ferry his kids up the mountain and back. He could have volunteered his time to employ his handyman skills fixing up a Christian camp on the weekends. He should have tested his vision for Christian camping through small "pilot projects" in which, had his vision not been of God, he could have failed quickly and easily rather than come crashing down like a large meteorite.

Start small, go deep, think big. If you're going to fail, fail quickly.

God Works through People

Frequently when we think of ministry we think of significant ministry structures, the big organizations. But the reality is that when ministry is accomplished—even in the big organizations—it is accomplished through people. And a big organization is not a prerequisite to effective ministry.

Dave Navarro grew up among the gangs of Southern California's San Fernando Valley. He knew firsthand the poverty, hopelessness, and violence that characterized the lives of young Latino males struggling for identity and self-esteem.

In the midst of this background, in 1971, Dave came to know Christ as his Savior. He married, secured a good job, and became a father. He began attending The Church on the Way. For many, the story would have ended here—his life with the gangs behind him.

After being a member of The Church on the Way for nearly fifteen years, Dave got involved with one of the church's "World Teams." He was considering a ministry as a missionary, but he couldn't shake a very specific burden for his hometown of Pacoima. Dave relates how, as he was praying for Pacoima one day, the Lord led his thoughts to the fourth chapter of John, and the story of Christ's meeting the woman at the well. "As I read through this story, I saw that Christ was a well, overflowing with living water for the people whose lives he touched. The Lord then said to me, 'I would like your ministry to be a well, overflowing with Christ's living water for the people in Pacoima.'" At the time, Dave was unaware that the name *Pacoima* was a Native American word that meant *flowing waters.*

Dave had no money for a facility, but in thinking about where people gathered in Pacoima, he realized that he would be more likely to find a suitable audience at a large, central park—"a logical place for a well to be located."

The first thing that Dave and his small group of World Team volunteers did was to begin collecting modest amounts of food and clothing, taking it into the park on Saturday mornings for distribution to those who evidenced a need. "It was important to us, though, not simply to meet their physical needs, but to meet their spiritual needs as well. So after we had passed out the food and clothing, we would walk among the people and ask them if they had any needs we could pray for." The entire ministry revolved around three simple activities—distributing food and clothing, singing songs of worship, and praying with the people in the park.

Almost unintentionally, the effort grew rapidly, attracting both new volunteers and large numbers of needy people. Soon Dave's team had swelled to nearly two hundred people who were distributing, worshipping, and praying.

After three Saturday mornings, the park had grown so crowded that city park officials, who had difficulty finding a parking space, began to take notice. The supervisor, a kindly fellow by the name of Joe, told Dave, "We appreciate what you're doing and we're sympathetic. You can feed people in the park, but because of the separation of church and state, you can't pray with them here."

Dave didn't want to put up a fight, even though he felt the supervisor's fears were groundless, so he brainstormed a way to work around the limitation. After feeding and clothing people within the park, the team members would take the people who wanted prayer onto the public sidewalk. Soon the sidewalk surrounding the park was filled with praying people, which attracted even larger crowds. (Eventually Dave reapproached the parks department with a request to allow them to pray inside the park. This time he met with no resistance. It turned out that the group's reputation had filtered to high places, and the supervisor himself had received a commendation from a member of the county board of supervisors, for the good work that was going on in "his" park!)

It wasn't long before the park ministry in Pacoima began to form what Dave calls a "community," which was in reality a budding church. They began meeting for prayer on weeknights at the homes of various people from Pacoima whom they'd met in the park. Soon these individuals, members of Dave's community, found that they themselves had become the "ministers" by feeding their neighbors in their local park. Dave and his team of two hundred volunteers from The Church on the Way spent their time leading worship and seeking to meet spiritual needs.

The Pacoima Outreach, as it was called, soon became a church in its own right, and in the spirit of its own founding has now begun to reach out to other communities as well. Several other outreaches have begun in the San Fernando Valley as a result. Renato Vasques, a member of the original team, serves as pastor.

Three facts mark the unique success of the Pacoima Outreach in meeting the needs of this ministry:

- Dave responded to a consistent vision from the Lord. He has been true to the theme of "living waters," which the Lord originally gave him.
- He does not erect any artificial barrier between the Great Commandment and the Great Commission. Evangelism flows directly out of meeting people's needs. As a result of the outreach, about fifty people per month come to know the Lord. ("We documented that carefully for the first three years," Dave says, "then it got to be too much for us and we gave up.") There is some street preaching but it is not overtly evangelistic. In spite of this, multitudes are coming to the Lord.
- Dave utilizes those to whom he seeks to minister to actually do ministry to others. When they began a new outreach, he went to a street that was notorious as being the turf of a tough gang. The team boldly approached the gang's leaders, saying, "We have all this food that we want to give out to people on your street. Will you help us by passing the word and helping us distribute the food?" They got the gang members working for the team instead of against them, and the ministry flourished.

Dave was willing to start small, in a park. He didn't ask for huge amounts of money or other types of resources, but did what he could with what he had on hand.

Seven Advantages of Pilot Projects

1. Pilot projects are a "college education" for the minister who would make a "career" of implementing ideas on a larger scale. If the idea is solid, a few team members are on board, it is backed by a good strategic plan, and God is behind the idea, the pilot project will always be rewarded with success.
2. It is easy to get permission for pilot projects. It may be difficult to get your pastor to back you if you approach him or her and say, "I need $10,000, fifty volunteers, and the use of three church buses to distribute food to hungry people in our city." But if you approach the pastor and say, "I'm planning to take my wife and kids down to skid row and pass out a few bags of groceries—would you pray for me?"—well, what pastor

could or would want to say no to that? And if in passing out the groceries you are able to develop some relationships with the people on the street and you return the next night with some blankets, and the night after that with clothing and eventually someone gets saved and people from your church get excited about joining you—well, then, that's a different story. You can earn a hearing from those who are in the position to grant permissions simply by taking your idea and implementing it on a small scale and, then, carefully documenting its success.

3. Pilot projects will generate success stories that can later be used to give vision to volunteers (human resources), and to generate material or financial resources.

4. "Modeling" is a crucial leadership quality, and the pilot project is an opportunity for you to model for others the type of behavior that is desirable and necessary in order to meet the needs of your target population.

5. Pilot projects enable ideas to "fail gracefully," and to fail in a way that isn't fatal. George Bernard Shaw wrote, "Anything worth doing is worth doing wrong." If you expend huge amounts of resources on a project and it fails, you've disappointed a lot of people. However, if a small pilot project fails, then you simply chalk it up as a learning experience. If the idea doesn't work the first time, it can be tweaked as needed and retested through another pilot project, without losing a substantial investment of resources and without limiting the potential for additional resources.

6. Pilot projects shouldn't cost a lot, either in terms of human resources or materials or money. There's not a lot to lose. Don't go to a church board or staff committee requesting resources for a pilot project. If you have a vision for ministry, pray that God will supply what you need. Work quietly behind the scenes and use whatever he gives you to get the job done.

7. Pilot projects enable you to make on-the-fly adjustments to your strategic ministry plan. If a specific aspect of your ministry doesn't work, it's a simple matter at this point to make the change. Pilot projects take fullest advantage of the adage, "Ready! Fire! Aim!"

Ministry Partnerships

In addition, you may wish to explore partnerships with a larger number of churches (pooling meager resources), or with the business sector. Some of the most successful ministries operate as an interdependent partnership between the lay ministry, the church, and the business sector.

One example of such a ministry is the Door of Hope in Pasadena, California. Directed by Richard Howard, the Door of Hope is a discipleship-oriented shelter home in Pasadena ministering to entire families taken off the streets of Los Angeles and out of the city environment. It was begun in 1984 when Union Rescue Mission in Los Angeles began to notice that two-parent families with children were showing up on skid row. The goal of this home is an intensive discipleship and disciplined training regimen designed to retool these families for a productive role in society.

The home works with only four families at a time, in three-month cycles. Residents are closely supervised in the completion of classes, chores, and accountability assignments. Even free time is tightly orchestrated so that they are required to spend more productive time with their children than these parents are accustomed to doing. Meanwhile, volunteers from about one hundred local churches teach classes and bring in twenty-five evening potluck meals per month, which they sit down and enjoy with the home's residents.

This interdependency with local churches is just the beginning of the Door's partnering efforts. In addition to a close working relationship with the Union Rescue Mission and such other local agencies as the United Way, the Door of Hope works interdependently with local businesses: Steve Lazarian, the chairman of the board, is a successful businessman-contractor. One of his companies purchased the home that houses the families and rents it to the ministry. The business gets the tax break, the good publicity, and the privilege of serving its community; Door of Hope gets the home and an understanding landlord who shares their vision without the entanglements of owning hard assets like property. The home is also an investment for the company because it has increased in value since its purchase. Financially, Door of Hope is supported at 25 percent by local churches, 50 percent by individuals, and the remaining 25 percent from miscellaneous sources, including local businesses.

Writing in an article entitled "Community Partners," in the July/August 1992 issue of *The Christian Ministry*, Eugene Roehlepartain tells of another interesting innovation in church-ministry partnerships, taking place in Waterbury, Connecticut, where "more than 40 churches and 20 community organizations have joined together to promote local leadership development. In one initiative, the partnership has begun an employee-owned home health-care business to provide jobs for local workers and to serve the local community." Here in Los Angeles, development corporations created by two separate church congregations, one Latin American and the other African American, are creating a land trust for developing low-income housing in the riot-torn south-central portion of the city.

A company called Rainbow Research, Incorporated, based in Minneapolis, has published a report full of such examples of interdependent development partnerships between churches and their communities.[1]

Evaluating Your Field-Test

How do you evaluate a field-test? In chapter 5 we discussed the need to take frequent vital signs of your ministry's health. Some of these vital signs can give important clues as to whether a ministry is succeeding or failing.

Goal Achievement. Is your ministry achieving its goals? This question presupposes, of course, that you have a way to measure whether or not your goals are being achieved. (If your ministry goals aren't measurable, then you shouldn't be doing ministry because true ministry always helps people, and that's always a measurable phenomenon.) If you can't point out a person who is being helped by your ministry, then chances are your pilot project has some problems.

Cost-effectiveness. Not only should you be achieving your goals; you should be achieving them within budget and in a manner that does not squander human, material, or financial resources. Make sure you keep a running balance sheet, or at least keep an eye on the checkbook balance. If your ministry is functioning substantially beyond budget, then there may be some serious adjustment needed.

Motivated Team Members. Is it easy for you to recruit *and keep* team members who are motivated by your vision for ministry? If your back door is swinging faster than your front door, then you may need to scrap the pilot project and go through the strategic planning process a second time.

Core Values and Mission Statement. Is ministry being conducted in a manner that reflects both your core values and your mission statement? If in the pilot project your ministry is straying too far from this centerline, it's time to reevaluate.

Reasonable Obstacles. Is your path smooth and trouble free, or are you experiencing occasional obstacles to ministry? *No effective ministry operates without facing obstacles;* that's not simply rhetoric, but an immutable scriptural principle dealing with our experience here on planet earth.

Replication. Is your ministry envied and emulated by others? A certain amount of recognition, even if it is grudging, usually comes to a healthy ministry that is bearing fruit. Replication is the highest form of flattery.

Bearing Fruit. Effective ministries will bear fruit. People will be reconciled to the Lord, wounds will be healed, lives will be turned around or saved, people will be given a renewed sense of dignity and worth. Christopher Adsit writes that only three things are eternal: God, the Word of God, and the souls of men.[2] If you can "spend what you cannot keep" in order to build up treasure in any one of these three areas, it's always a good exchange.

An evaluation of a pilot test's success or failure is an important event, and one that should not be confined to the perspective of a single individual. Be sure to get your team involved in the process, as well as others to whom you are accountable or whose wisdom you trust. Some of your judgments will be objective and some subjective; the final judgment that counts is the confirmation that you must receive from the Lord through prayer before proceeding.

Remember that there are always three options in responding to an evaluation:

1. The pilot test was an absolute success; proceed with the project as planned.
2. The pilot test was an abject failure; dump the entire thing and forget it ever happened.
3. The results are mixed; go back to the drawing board. Another cut at the strategic planning process may help produce a positive adjustment and prepare your ideas for another pilot run. Don't abandon. Rethink.

Obtaining Permissions

Let's say your field-test is a resounding success. What next? It's time to write a clear project proposal and obtain the necessary permissions to operate your strategic ministry on a larger scale.

Getting Your Church to Embrace Your Ministry

Community Baptist Church had established about fifty cell groups and was basically learning how they worked. Ed Carey, a lay leader in our church, had a burden not simply to establish a cell group, but to establish a ministry group whose focus would be to redeem and use the Twelve Steps in support groups that would help free alcoholics, drug addicts, and their families from enslavement to their addictions.

You see, Ed was experiencing a passion for ministry that had arisen from his own woundedness. In 1981 Ed was a successful businessman who had developed a very profitable feed and grain operation, then sold it for over one million dollars—cash. He needed these funds to finance another venture—his growing love affair with cocaine and alcohol.

About this same time Ed's wife, Lou, came to Community Baptist Church as a new Christian looking for a church home. At the church she discovered not only a family of people that supported and encouraged her in the midst of her marital crisis, but one that was also willing to offer concrete help by giving her a secretarial job in the church office.

As a result of some severe legal problems caused by Ed's drug habit, Lou filed for a legal separation in 1982. During their separation Lou prayed for God's truth to penetrate Ed's life.

It took Ed about three years of wild living to finally hit bottom. It was Thanksgiving of 1984 when he found himself penniless and in a jail cell with several outstanding warrants. Having gone through the torment of withdrawal in his prison cell, Ed now faced his own loneliness and desolation. Then Ed's Christian cellmate showed him the way to the foot of the cross, where he knelt to receive Christ as his Savior.

With God's help, Ed began the difficult task of trying to put his life and family back together. He wrote a letter to Lou and she visited him in jail, where they talked about the possibility of reconciliation. Lou was hopeful, but cautious; this was what she had prayed for during the three years of separation. After six weeks of talking and praying, Lou made arrangements to have Ed released from jail on bail and brought him home in time for Christmas.

The family was back together, but there were still many legal problems that had to be worked through as a result of Ed's drug and alcohol days. He had to go to court on the outstanding warrants. Ed's attorney advised him to expect to spend time in jail, but through the grace of God he was given a suspended sentence and placed on parole.

There was also the problem of taxes on the sale of Ed's business. In consulting with tax specialists and attorneys it became evident that the government would never find out about the sale of the business. Many advised Ed to simply forget about filing tax returns showing the sale. Ed and Lou prayed over this advice and looked to the Bible for answers. After reading, "If you owe taxes, pay taxes," they decided to file.

With penalties, the final figure showed a tax liability of over one million dollars. Ed had gone from having one million dollars in cash, to a debt in excess of that amount. But the government was willing to work out a payment plan, and then in 1991, through another miracle of God, the debt was totally discharged.

During this process, as Ed reflected on his life and ministry, he realized that his debt went beyond what he owed to the government. He had been dealing with his addiction to alcohol and drugs by leading a group using a Christian version of the Alcoholics Anonymous Twelve Step program. The group was struggling for direction when he heard about another Christian recovery group in Whittier, California, called Overcomers.[3] After visiting the group he knew this was the answer to his prayers.

Ed had many friends who needed the healing that was available through the Overcomers program, and he also saw this group as a potential way to help his friends come to know the Lord and assimilate them into the life of the church. He knew that Overcomers was right for CBC, and so his task was to sell its benefits to the church's leadership and help them see how the group would help the church achieve its own goals.

I started by looking at CBC's core values. I knew that the church had a value of reaching out to hurting people in our community. This group would do that. It valued introducing the previously unchurched, through "fishing-pool events," into the life of the church and thus to the Lord. I believed the Overcomers could do that. It valued discipleship, the maturing of both new and old believers. This group would do that.

But where I really saw the potential for success was in the value of reproducing groups. Could Overcomers become a reproducing group? I believed it could, and I set about to conduct it so that it would.

The Overcomers reproduced itself within our own church. Ed mentored and discipled a number of leaders who came up through the ranks. They became the leaders of a diverse spread of daughter Overcomers groups. Soon the network was too big to be confined within CBC's walls, and so Ed began planting Overcomers groups in other churches as well. He became a key reproducing leader in the Southern California network of Overcomers groups.

The pastoral staff at CBC, who have demonstrated the ability to acknowledge and affirm success, even when it is unexpected, slapped Ed on the back and acknowledged his achievement by offering him a staff position at the church—director of Recovery Ministries. He wanted to share the directorship, including its modest stipend, with at least one apprentice. The deal was done, and Percell Maynard, one of Ed's "wounded healers" who had demonstrated a superior ability and commitment to ministering to others, was chosen for the job of administrator.

Percell now directs an aspect of CBC's Recovery Ministry known as Community-Oriented Drug Education, Incorporated (CODE). CODE's focus is on providing a homelike recovery environment for men and women whose lives have been destroyed by drugs. Needy individuals stay in one of CODE's sober living homes for an average of six months, undergoing an intensive program of discipleship and recovery.

Writing a Clear Ministry Proposal

A ministry proposal will be a necessary part of any presentation to a church board or committee. Every ministry proposal should be an elaboration of your statement of mission, and should answer the following questions:[4]

1. Why start this ministry? Demonstrate the need for this ministry, and briefly share your calling (passion) and vision.
2. Who is the target group on whom this ministry will focus? Describe the characteristics of the target group you have selected. Include demographics data, where appropriate, to show that you have done your homework.
3. What kind of ministry are you seeking to establish? Articulate your core values. State and expand on your mission statement. Present your completed ministry flowchart.
4. With whom will you start this ministry? Describe the roles and functions required on your team, and include a profile of who is already in place to fulfill those roles and functions.
5. What is your strategy in developing this ministry? Write out your three- to five-year goals. Draw a detailed time line for the first year (can be taken from your Post-it planning), and include cash-flow projections and start-up budget. Define your funding strategy and describe how volunteers may be involved. Detail all:

   - Prayer needs
   - Volunteer needs
   - Potential contacts
   - Equipment needs
   - Financial needs

6. Identify key decisions that still need to be made, along with your time line for making them, to show that you have covered all the bases in your strategic planning.
7. Give very specific information on precisely what you are asking of the body to whom you are making the ministry proposal. Exactly what do you expect from them? Financial support? How much, and when? Volunteers? Material resources? Prayer support? Or merely affirmation and moral support?

If you need more help in understanding how to work with leaders so that they endorse a new ministry, refer to the chapter "Obtaining Goal Ownership" in *Leading and Managing Your Church* (Grand Rapids: Fleming H. Revell, 1987) by Bob Logan and Carl George.

Ongoing Issues

Promote and Communicate Your Ministry

One of the biggest ongoing challenges confronting ministry leaders is keeping the vision in front of people:

- volunteers and staff
- permission-givers and resource-providers
- intercessors
- potential volunteers and donors
- the "general public" in your community or church—whether that public is represented by a local newspaper, church newsletter, radio station, or mailing list

Vision cannot simply be presented once and then left alone. It must be reiterated and re-presented constantly, in ever new and creative ways, in order to continue to get people's attention and expand the scope of your ministry to more individuals.

Communicating an ongoing vision is absolutely necessary if you are to:

- Recruit additional workers (never be satisfied with what you have because of the constant potential for volunteer turnover and the demands of ministry growth)
- Discover sources of assistance, referrals, and ministry allies (among churches, business, the community at large, and other ministry organizations)
- Develop additional contacts with key people within your ministry target group (for expanding the base of your ministry)
- Develop additional funding (to meet the needs of ministry growth)
- Increase your base of prayer support (for greater blessing and effectiveness)

How do you keep your vision fresh and sharp?

- Keep close to the people to whom you are ministering. Make sure you don't get numb, but that your own heart remains broken to their plight and to the plight of those you cannot yet reach.

- Look for personal stories that will touch the hearts of those with whom you communicate. Religiously write down success stories, and file them away for future use!

- Keep lifting up the vision in prayer before the Lord. Meditate on Scripture that relates to your vision. Ask God to do for you what he did for Jabez—to ever expand your borders and enable you to see more of his heart and his blessing for your ministry.

- Remember that vision is an issue of the heart. Your heart must be right before God. You must be continually renewing your own vision with times of Sabbath rest. Take care for your own soul. If you burn out physically, mentally, emotionally, or spiritually, then the flame of vision dies out with you. Your ministry structure may continue for some time, but it will be an empty shell, grinding on without the empowerment of vision to keep it motivated. Eventually those around you will lose their vision, too, and the entire ministry will screech to a halt.

What are the most effective forums for communicating your vision to others?

The individual, face-to-face meeting. Schedule periodic lunch or breakfast appointments with key opinion leaders in your ministry, in your church, and in your community, to share your vision and your excitement over what God is doing in your ministry. This is a substantial investment of time and energy, but one that will pay large dividends and earn many allies.

Face-to-face group communication. The effective ministry leader will develop requisite speaking skills and the ability to present his or her vision to groups of people at church meetings, small-group meetings, community forums, and meetings of your own team. Time-management experts complain that not a lot of business is effectively accomplished at face-to-face meetings; so limit the agenda—take care of the business details in other settings. But the most important thing that must happen, which cannot happen any other way than through frequent meetings of your team, is the "catching" of a leader's vision for ministry. (The second most important thing is to affirm your team members and give time for the entire team to listen to their perspective.) Remember the key biblical principle that heart ownership follows investment of resources. Today, the time required for meetings represents a significant investment. Use the time wisely and well to stoke the fires of enthusiasm and vision.

The telephone. The ads on TV are right; the telephone is a much neglected instrument that can accomplish a great deal for the leader who will use it wisely and well. Setting aside an evening for telephone calls to key individuals will always strengthen your ministry. Calls should be upbeat and enthusiastic. Inform about ministry developments and enlist their prayer support and their help in telling others. Give ownership and delegate tasks. If you are disciplined you can accomplish in a fifteen-minute call what might take an hour-long face-to-face meeting.

Newsletters and support letters. Every successful ministry effort needs to develop a mailing list of prayer supporters, financial supporters, potential supporters, permission givers, and other interested parties. It is worth your while to expend whatever energy it takes to keep your list as "clean" as possible because mailing costs per address can be exorbitant over the period of a year. Many beginning ministries will find a list of fifty or one hundred names to be sufficient if those people are committed to your ministry. And this list will, of course, grow as your organization grows. With modern desktop computers, newsletters and letters that look very nice can be produced by committed volunteers with relative ease. Newsletters need not be extremely complex—just two or four pages of clean text with a few photos or graphics sprinkled in to break things up. You may wish to limit the more expensive newsletters to once every two to three months, and send out a simpler support letter more frequently. Focus your energy in the support letter not merely on informing, but to sharing vision with your readers. Always tell a heart-touching success story, when you can, to help your readers visualize the person-to-person nature of your ministry.

Ongoing Ministry Success

Janet Logan shares, from her ministry experience, three critical components for the ongoing success of ministry:

Remember that listening is an ongoing process. Keep your fingers on the pulse of your community, and on the broader aspects of your ministry's role in society.

- Continue to conduct interviews with people who can give you greater insights into the needs of your target group as well as current efforts to meet those needs.
- Subscribe to relevant publications, both those that are specific to your ministry area and those with broader focus. For the local picture, subscribe to local newspapers and the newsletters of other ministry efforts. Ask others who read widely to be on the lookout for articles relevant to your ministry. Clip any that you find and distribute to your team members.
- Don't fear change, but let your attitude be one of embracing it!

Strengthen relationships with your coworkers.

- Develop a network of peers—leaders of other ministries similar to your own. Meet with them regularly to pray and share ideas and information.
- Continue to strengthen friendships and working relationships with your team members. Be sure to consider them your peers as well. Keep working on discipleship and mentoring relationships. Be sure to have one or two individuals you are continually grooming to take your place.

Continue working on your personal growth issues. Don't neglect the importance of continual character development. Your character is the "goose" that you must keep healthy in order to keep the "golden eggs" of quality leadership coming.

- Guard yourself against burnout. Schedule and treasure your Sabbath rests, and seek a continual renewal of vision from the Lord.
- Maintain the other priorities in your life—your family (spouse, children); other church fellowship, worship, and ministry activities; recreation; friendships. Too often impassioned ministry leaders are so single-mindedly focused on their task that they forget that they are human beings who need a balanced life

that includes regular meals, sleep, and human relationships to keep them going!

Action Idea Checklist

- ☐ Ask the Lord for guidance, wisdom, and strength as you serve compassionately.
- ☐ Conduct appropriate pilot projects before launching major ministry efforts; pre-determine how to measure the effectiveness of the pilot.
- ☐ Build a team of advisors to help evaluate ministry effectiveness.
- ☐ Develop a clear strategy to obtain necessary permissions and increase ownership of your ministry.
- ☐ Cultivate a personal support system for encouragement, counsel, and accountability.
- ☐ Network with other people, churches, and organizations to increase the potential of compassionate service to others.

Add your own follow-up items below.

7

Equipping Leaders for Maximum Effectiveness

There are many metaphors that describe effective leaders. One that our society is well acquainted with is that of a coach. In spite of the abundance of coaches with whom we are acquainted, however, very few understand the real nature of coaching. When asked, "What makes a good coach?" we say, "His or her team wins." That is true, but it does not answer the question. Winning is simply one indication that the coach is doing something right. It is a symptom of good coaching. But why is the coach of a winning team a good coach? What is it about the process of good coaching that increases the likelihood that one's team will win?

Five Steps to Effective Coaching

Steve Ogne and Bob Logan developed the following coaching model as a result of many years of experience coaching ministry leaders, pastors, and church planters.

Listen Empathetically

Seek first to understand. Frequently we have the perception that a coach is one who spends his time yelling instructions at his players, "Keep your eye on the ball, Johnson!" However, the true function of a coach is not simply to direct his team, but to understand their strengths and weaknesses, to discern how their attitudes at any given time affect their performance, and how to motivate them. In order to do this, one must not simply yell, but one must first listen. Good coaches apply Stephen Covey's fifth habit of highly effective people—they seek to understand before seeking to be understood.

Get inside the player's frame of reference. How does your team member perceive the ministry? What motivates him? Does he enjoy and feel fulfilled by what he is doing? Is he frustrated? What significance does he assign his service in the context of the rest of his life? Answer these types of questions for each of your team members.

If you have a point to make—a skill to teach, a word of advice, an opinion to proffer—see if you can't do it from within the player's frame of reference. We listen to people when we sense that they truly understand us and are concerned about our point of view. If we demonstrate that we understand their point of view as well as they do, then we earn an audience for our own.

Use your ears, eyes, and heart. Empathetic listening uses more than just one's ears and mind. Social scientists tell us that 80 percent of what we communicate is nonverbal. In a personal interaction, study a team member's gestures, facial expression, and body posture for clues to how that person feels about what is being discussed. And use your heart as well. As you are listening, be praying, *Lord, please help me understand where this person is coming from. Help me to empathize, to see things from within his or her frame of reference. Let our communication be heart-to-heart.*

Care Personally

Effective coaches win the allegiance of their players, not simply by caring about their performance on the team, but by caring about them personally. They understand that a person's life is significant in more ways than simply their role on the team.

Respond to needs. Nothing can destroy a trusting relationship like ignoring a hurt. We've all had times of heartache when we desired to share that with another person. We're not at our most pleasant when we have to communicate while in pain. How that person with whom we are sharing responds, can make all the difference in the world. If he or she responds in anger or tunes us out, our pain is magnified with a new hurt—the thought that others simply don't care. But if the response is nonjudgmental listening and an earnest desire to help share our burden, our load is immediately lightened. When you're carrying a heavy burden, whether it is ten pounds or a hundred, if someone takes half of that burden, there is immediate relief. Suddenly what we have seems more bearable, and our strength is renewed.

The most caring and effective leaders respond immediately to the needs of others in the same way that they respond when confronted by a great personal burden—they take it straight to the throne of God. Too often, after listening to someone express a need, we feel compelled to prescribe. We right away offer advice from our own autobiographies. "When that happened to me I did thus and thus." "Have you tried thus and thus?" We haven't taken time to diagnose. And for us Christians, the critical issue in diagnosis is praying over a need, seeking the Lord's wisdom.

Respond to emotion. Romans 12:15 advises, "Rejoice with those who rejoice; mourn with those who mourn." In our impersonal culture we are too often afraid to reach out and comfort someone with a touch or a hug. Yet such small favors are good medicine. Studies show that newborn babies who are showered with loving touch are much healthier than those who are denied this comfort. Sharing a laugh, a hug, or a tear is a cleansing experience that communicates care and affirmation to our Christian brothers and sisters.

Refer as needed. Seeking to care for people's needs can be a humbling process; we will soon realize how much we don't know, and we must be willing to admit this to others. Part of the process of caring will be helping others get in touch with people or resources that can help them in their need. Every ministry leader should keep a referral directory at his fingertips, knowing who the experts are who can help out a brother or a sister in a given area of need. And remember to honor the trust that you are given by exercising great caution to guard as confidential all sensitive needs that are expressed to you.

Celebrate Victories

Good coaches know how to party! They know where the so-called ledges are on the climb to the peak where the team can relax, recuperate, rejuvenate, and celebrate. And they know how to use celebration as a tool of affirmation of their players' gifts, skills, and character. There are two types of celebrations that should be intentionalized in your ministry.

Progress—Celebrate all milestones toward the achievement of your ministry's goals. Use each celebration to reaffirm your organization's vision, and to help team members see their own role in achieving that vision.

Personal achievement—When a team member has achieved a personal goal or experienced a personal victory, celebration and affirmation are in order! Remembering birthdays, anniversaries, and other special occasions is a way to keep affirming the intrinsic value of each person and his or her contribution to the team.

Strategize Plans

Effective coaches know the importance of the huddle. The huddle is a time before the play in which everyone's attention is completely and intensely focused on the game plan. Here are some important things that happen in the huddle.

Focus priorities. "Here is where we are, the fifty yard line, and here is where we'd like to be—in the end zone. Our first priority in the next play will be to get the ball into the hands of Johnson, who can run it down there." The coach should have a unique perspective on the game—the "big picture." While the plays are being run, he or she is sitting back and evaluating, thinking through the implications of individual actions and how they exhibit the potential to achieve the objective. It is out of that perspective that the coach must act to focus the team's priorities.

Eliminate roadblocks. The coach must identify the obstacles to be overcome and figure out how to achieve this. "Myers, you sack that defensive end; put him right on his fanny, okay?"

Maximize resources. In any ministry, there is a finite quantity of resources—human, material, and financial. Therefore, they must be rationed. Allocation of resources must be carefully thought out, so that the most effective strategies are rewarded with the highest investment of resources. "Smith and Jones, you two have to focus on protecting that center. If we can buy him the time to get that ball to the quarterback, then we stand a chance."

Determine the next step. Since the best and most complex strategic plans always break down to "one step at a time," the job of the coach, in looking at the overall picture, is to understand where the team is at any given time and to know and communicate what the next step in ministry is. The people in the trenches don't always see this; their activities may be sporadic and stopgap simply because they can't see the forest for the trees. The coach is the one to say,

"Okay, it's first down and fifty to go. The next step is to run the ball around a bit. It's not quite the right time to kick."

Challenge Specifically

So often, when it comes to working with our team, we have not because we ask not. We are afraid to ask our own people to set challenging goals and give us greater performance. When meeting with a team member and delegating tasks, be sure to accomplish each of the following three objectives:

Clarify vision and goals. Asking, "What are we here to do?" is essential to any interaction in which your team members are challenged to greater achievement. The quest for meaning is a central human motivator. If your people understand the need to reach for the stars, if they're trained how to do it and challenged specifically, you're going to get the stars. Challenging your team members to greater achievement affirms your belief in their capacity to achieve the team's goals, and stimulates them to greater effort. Set a high standard for your team members to work toward, a mark to shoot for.

Determine next steps and assignments. Any goal is achievable if it can be broken down into an uninterrupted series of smaller, doable steps. Most college students at the end of the first week of their freshman year are terrified by the immensity of the task before them. And yet, as every senior understands, large achievements are possible given sufficient time and the steadfast achievement of the proper sequence of steps toward the goal. Specifically, who is going to do what, and by when? Write it down and give each person a copy.

Set the next meeting. People are motivated by accountability to a deadline. The fact is, for most people, 80 percent of the effort required to achieve a goal will be expended in the final 20 percent of the time remaining until the deadline. Make sure the deadline is realistic and fully owned by the team member you are meeting with. When setting appointments, give careful consideration to the need to set a "soft" deadline with a sufficient buffer of time separating it from the "hard" deadline (the absolute time by which a task should be completed). This built-in buffer can then serve as an added measure of grace in case the team member runs into difficulties completing the task.

Conducting "Coaching" Sessions

The following is a suggested agenda for meeting with your team members.

1. Find out how each is doing personally. Exercise and model empathetic-listening skills and use the first portion of your time to express care for the needs of your team member.
2. Determine progress on current projects. Use your Post-it planning boards and debrief the team member on the status of each project he or she is working on. Focus priorities, eliminate roadblocks, maximize resources, and determine the next steps.
3. Give encouragement for positive achievement. Celebrate victories.
4. Discover current needs and/or priorities. What resources are needed to successfully complete the tasks at hand? How is your team member prioritizing those tasks?
5. Ask appropriate questions to clarify next steps.
6. Agree on and write down on the Post-it planning board specific assignments. Agree on time lines, milestones, and how success will be measured.
7. Pray with and for your leaders.

Six Keys for Developing Leaders

Assessment—Determine gifting, abilities, interests, passion, personality, commitment, energy, and time available.

Assignment—Give specific task assignments that are challenging, yet attainable. Design the level of difficulty around the team member and his or her skills and experience. Christ discipled using a sequential process of ever more challenging steps; think through the progression of tasks you are assigning to ensure that the level of challenge steadily and consistently increases.

Assistance—Provide vision, adequate resources, and consistent support for your team members to stand on as they seek to achieve each task.

Accountability—Schedule regular reviews in which to evaluate experiences, summarize results, and discern areas for improvement.

Applause—Acknowledge your team members' unique contributions; affirm their intrinsic value to the team and celebrate all victories.

Advancement—Create and provide continuing opportunities for personal and professional growth, renewal, and challenge.

Consistently Cast Vision

We've spoken at length about the challenge of keeping before your team the vision for your ministry. The primary responsibility for this task will fall on your shoulders, and yours alone. As the "vision caster" for your ministry, you must:

- Paint a picture of the benefits of your ministry's achieving its ministry goals at various points in the future
- Develop and expound a consistent theme that highlights the vision and your philosophy of ministry
- Be the salesman for your vision, selling it continually to your team members as well as others observing your ministry
- Approach challenges as opportunities instead of obstacles
- Effectively prevent or neutralize the efforts of those who would throw a "wet blanket" on your ministry vision
- Guard against erecting artificial walls that limit the abilities of God or the capacities of yourself or your team members
- Establish a clear "ministry identity," incorporating your vision and theme
- Propagate belief in God's ability to accomplish great things through your ministry[1]

One of the greatest mistakes many ministry leaders make is a lack of effective communication, primarily with team members and ministry observers-supporters. Leaders underestimate the importance of regular letters, calls, and newsletters. They do not schedule a sufficient number of vision-casting events, such as banquets or retreats. Team members and supporters all need to be continually reenergized with the vision of the organization and reports of its progress. They need to hear success stories and be exposed to your ongoing passion for ministry.

Dynamics of Ministry Systems

Much of this book has focused on innovation in ministry—how do you start something that will meet people's needs? But innovation is only half the story. The next question to ask is, how do you take a functional ministry that is basically achieving its goals, and make it work better?

We've all heard the old saying, "If it ain't broke, don't fix it." But in the case of ministry structures, many times the best time to work on fixing your ministry (in the sense of making it better), is when things are going well for you. Why is this?

Too often we wait until we are in the midst of crisis to attempt to make significant changes. But this is like attempting a science experiment with too many variables. In order to effectively evaluate the results of your tinkering, you need a control sample against which to compare the sample that you have experimented on. In the case of making changes to your ministry, the best control is a normally functioning, healthy ministry that isn't in the midst of some crisis. If you make changes in a ministry that is functioning well, and it begins to function better, then there is a strong likelihood that the improvement was the result of the change you've made. But if your ministry is in flux, and you make a change and it improves, you cannot know for sure whether the improvement was actually the result of your change or not. In that case your hypothesis remains inadequately tested.

So, when your ministry is running at "cruising speed" and performing up to expectation, when things seem relatively stable, this is the time to begin to evaluate your ministry in light of possible improvements. Here are some questions to ask:

- How is each area of ministry contributing to our goal? Which areas are contributing most significantly?
- Are there other ministries we are aware of (or can be made aware of) that are seeking to meet similar needs in different ways? What is their experience? How can we network with them to learn from them?
- Which ministry areas consume the greatest amount of human, material, or financial resources? Are these areas the same ones that are experiencing the best success?
- Where would you draw a "discard line" on the following chart, dumping unproductive or costly ministry activities?
- How would you work to move all remaining activities into quadrant 2? Brainstorm possible improvements, focusing on innovations that might replace costliness in human, material, or financial resources.

Evaluating Ministry Effectiveness

High Cost High Productivity	Low Cost High Productivity
Quadrant 1	Quadrant 2
Quadrant 3	Quadrant 4
High Cost Low Productivity	Low Cost Low Productivity

After brainstorming possible improvements, go through a Post-it strategic planning process, complete with the requisite reality checks (see chapter 5).

All effective ministry systems are reproducible; that is, there is a method by which someone (other than you) could come in, learn the ministry system, take it elsewhere, and make it work under similar circumstances.

Why are reproducible systems important? The main reason is human frailty. There are natural, built-in limits to the amount of ministry that one person can do. However, if ministry systems are designed to be reproducible, then the ministry leaders proactively seek to reproduce those systems; the ministry potential of one visionary person has therefore been multiplied manyfold. Reproducibility is the key and the genius behind the rise in fast-food restaurants like Ray Kroc's McDonald's hamburger chain. Kroc would never have been able to achieve the same results—the now-beyond-counting billions of hamburgers served in dozens of nations throughout the world—had he been content with flipping the burgers himself, and had he not designed a system to reproduce the success of McDonald's elsewhere.

The fact is, most ministries and many churches depend on the genius and/or expertise of the key leader for their success. The potential effectiveness and scope of this ministry is thereby limited by what the key leader can do by himself or herself, or can directly supervise. If on the way to work one morning a cement truck overturns and buries the ministry leader under ten tons of quick-dry cement, you might as well bury the ministry too.

The first step is deciding that you do not want your ministry to be totally dependent on you as leader. You have to have the humility and the vision to be willing and able to release control.

Second, you need to be willing to invest time and energy developing systems with built-in training and motivational aspects, systems that will empower your volunteers to do ministry and expand that ministry beyond the limits of your personal capacity.

The beauty of well-designed, reproducible ministry systems is that they:

- Empower ordinary people to do extraordinary things
- Increase the growth potential of your ministry
- Multiply your outreach without sacrificing quality control
- Allow a ministry to function properly, as it should
- Free leaders to lead rather than to "produce"

The best time to begin work on reproducible ministry systems is when your ministry is coasting, when it is doing consistently well. Here's how you begin:

1. Make sure you have an up-to-date diagram of your ministry systems process, or a Ministry Flowchart. For instructions on the design of a flowchart, see chapter 5. The purpose of designing a second flowchart, around what is already working, is that you will use it to "streamline" your ministry and focus on the aspects of it God is blessing.

    Remember that a comprehensive strategy for meeting a need must have multiple systems in place, various steps in the process of meeting that need (taking the person you are serving from one level to the next in logical sequence). These systems must be linked on paper if they are to be effective. That way, you and your team members can understand the linkages between each ministry area.

2. Second, define your job responsibilities. Write a job description for each team member that details responsibilities, lays

out requisite skills, and defines relationships through an organizational chart.

3. Define your procedures. Use a checklist format. Group, in separate areas on a checklist, standards of performance and specific tasks that must be accomplished.

Compiling these various documents—your updated ministry flowchart, job descriptions-organizational chart, and procedural checklists—into a comprehensive Operations Manual is the first critical step toward making a ministry reproducible. From this point on reproducibility becomes an issue of:

Modeling—Why would anyone else want to establish a ministry that meets needs in the manner yours does? Are you modeling an effective ministry structure?

Leadership—Pray that God will raise up leaders who will take your reproducible ministry systems and work with them to ensure their success.

Releasing—Like individual Christians and churches, effective ministries must be willing to give of themselves for the sake of others, raised up to follow in their footsteps. You may be called on to release your own ministry leaders or other resources to the new endeavor.

Treasure Your Greatest Treasure

Envision operating a ministry with no money—just dedicated, hard-working volunteers. Things might be difficult, but not, in most cases, impossible. Then try to envision operating a ministry with no volunteers, just money. It's easy to see that the most valuable resource for any ministry endeavor is its volunteers. Yet, it is the very resource that many ministries seem most willing to carelessly squander.

Your ministry will inevitably lose people. Their needs, interest, and passion will grow and change. For many ministries, there seems to be a burnout cycle of two to three years. But how do you minimize the potential loss of people? How do you design a ministry where people will be valued and their contributions cherished? How do you design their training to meet their deep-felt need for meaning?

Training That Lasts

Effective training recognizes a fundamental human principle. As human beings, we best learn a skill or a truth when we first feel or understand the need for that skill or truth.

This fact is basic and widely misunderstood. And yet, it is one of the most fundamentally ignored truths in education. How are Americans educated? They are sent to schools that sit their students down in a lecture hall and try to cram their heads with tons and tons of theory. Pastors go through years of schooling and learn all sorts of things without really understanding what it is that they most need to understand. After the schooling is completed they are thrust into a job setting where they suddenly begin to log the experiences that they needed training for. The problem is, they may or may not have received the specific training needed, and if they did, they didn't realize how seriously they needed it, and therefore didn't pay sufficient attention. In spite of being the culmination of many years of schooling, seminary education often fails to prepare a pastor for 60 percent of the things that he or she really needs to know.

But Christ trained his disciples far differently. He trained them not by sending them to school in advance, but by making the doing of ministry double as the schooling that they needed. His training was what we call just-in-time training. One gets the sense in reading the Gospels that Christ often waited for his disciples to ask the right questions. "As he went along," they happened on situations that contained lessons for the disciples, like the man born blind (John 9:1–6). When the disciples' curiosity was stimulated, they asked questions, and the situation was turned into a learning event for them.

Christ's Model: Orient, Involve, Equip

Our usual way is backward from the model that Christ demonstrated—*orient, involve, equip.*

Orient is not a full-blown training. It is simply establishing the framework. It is sharing the vision for a ministry, establishing a common understanding of principles, values, mission statement, and ministry method. It is Christ saying, "Follow Me, and I will make you fishers of men."

Involve recognizes the fact that the most effective training is on-the-job training. Those whom we would train must begin as apprentices.

- Being with and watching their mentor do real ministry in real-life situations.
- Doing ministry alongside their mentor, with close supervision and continual guidance.
- Doing ministry alone, but while the mentor sits back and watches, with thorough debriefing afterward.
- Being sent out by the mentor to complete a ministry task, and returning to debrief after it is completed.

Equip is the debriefing phase, after an apprentice has already been involved in ministry. It is at that point that the volunteer has the right questions to ask, and is in the correct mood to absorb the answers. Mark 9:14–29 tells the story of just such a teaching event in the disciples' lives.

A man brought to some of the disciples his son who was oppressed by a difficult demon. The disciples tried but couldn't cast it out. The man then appealed to Christ, who cast the demon out with a simple command. "You deaf and mute spirit," he said, "I command you, come out of him and never enter him again."

Afterwards, Christ debriefed his disciples in private. "Why couldn't we drive it out?" they asked. Jesus replied, "This kind can come out only by prayer."

Why did Christ wait until after their failure? Because he recognized the importance of capitalizing on teachable moments. Christ could have said, at the beginning of the three-year ministry, "Look, guys, sometimes casting out demons is tough. Sometimes you really need to pray first." The disciples would have nodded their heads and jotted another note in the margin, which then would have gone to the bottom of the cardboard box in the garage. It would have been wasted breath on Christ's part. But instead, he waited for a teachable moment.

Christ also recognized in his teaching that humans are creatures who learn best when the focus is narrow. Put one important truth in front of them, and keep it simple. "Pray first." Christ could have used the moment to dump another three tons of teaching about the nature of spiritual warfare, but he didn't; he just kept things simple and focused.

Use separate opportunities to teach separate skills. For instance, you might wish to design an exercise to teach the concept of empathetic listening. Ask the question: What is the one thing I want my apprentice to learn in this exercise? and plan the entire event around the answer to that one question. Design three or four different exercises that will drum in the same basic truth. Teach single skills starting with those that are most relevant and helpful in order for the apprentice to fulfill his or her part in achieving the team's vision. And then, practice immediate application. Skills can be learned and then easily lost if they are not practiced. Create or exploit opportunities for your apprentices to use, each day, the things that they are learning.

Developing Leaders

Your desire to develop your team members in their spiritual walk must first flow from the type of unconditional love that Christ exhibited for his disciples. He was willing, as a true friend, to "lay down his life" on their behalf. Moreover, as the lay leader of a ministry that requires a team approach for maximum effectiveness, you have a responsibility to disciple those under your tutelage, and you are in a very real sense taking on the "pastoral" responsibility of a small church. Many ministry leaders are prepared for the responsibility of ministering to their target group, but don't realize God calls them as well to minister to their team.

There are four essential steps in the process of developing your team members.

1. Help them clarify areas where God wants them to grow. Your evaluation of your team members should not be limited to merely their job performance, but should encompass their character as well.
2. Recommend appropriate Scripture and other helpful resources.
3. Assure them of your ongoing support, and build in periodic accountability and growth sessions.
4. Build an intercessory prayer base for yourself and encourage those you lead to do the same. All ministry leaders should have someone standing behind them, interceding for them in spiritual battle with those forces that would destroy the work of ministry. Intercessory prayer guards against "fatal" obstacles and

benefits the ministry leader by strengthening his godly will and protecting him against the possibility of moral failure.

Affirming Leaders

Janet Logan offers four simple ways that you can affirm the lay leaders who work under your supervision.

1. Provide continuing education opportunities. People are affirmed when we recognize the importance of their ongoing development. Remain aware of opportunities for ongoing education in their special area of deployment—conferences, seminars, classes—and encourage them to continually upgrade their education and polish their skills.
2. In order to encourage them to coach and train their workers, provide a small budget. Perhaps this would simply be $10 or $20 a month that would enable them to take their own apprentice out to lunch; but it affirms the importance of the training process and helps to turn them into teachers (who are the best learners).
3. Show an interest in their area of ministry specialty. Dr. Rob Acker, the pastor of Community Baptist Church, scours a number of publications, clipping articles that relate to the various ministry areas in the church and sending them to those leaders. He thus demonstrates a focused interest in them and their ministry, as well as in developing them and helping them to keep up-to-date.
4. Meet their needs. In many ministry environments, particularly in a church environment, one of the greatest needs is for creative ways to profile the needs of the ministry among the members of the church. This is something the pastor can provide for his ministry leaders at many different levels. Ask the right questions and find out what your ministry leaders' greatest frustrations are; then brainstorm with them and develop creative ways to help meet those needs.

Action Idea Checklist

☐ Ask God to help you effectively lead others—through modeling, coaching, vision casting, developing, and affirming.
☐ Find someone who can meet with you regularly for encouragement, and to focus action plans.

☐ Evaluate your skills as a coach and determine how you can improve.

☐ Make sure that everyone serving in ministry receives consistent coaching.

☐ Provide ongoing training and opportunities for character development.

☐ Design and implement reproducible systems.

Add your own follow-up items below.

𝒞onfronting Obstacles to Ministry

"Leadership is a foul weather job," says Peter Drucker. The times when we really need good leaders are when things are at their most difficult. Some of history's greatest leaders, men like Winston Churchill and Abraham Lincoln, made their mark in times of serious trouble.

> Fortunately or unfortunately, the one predictable thing in any organization is the crisis. That always comes.
> The most important task of an organization's leader is to anticipate crisis. Perhaps not to avert it, but to anticipate it. To wait until the crisis hits is already abdication. One has to make the organization capable of anticipating the storm, weathering it, and in fact, being ahead of it . . . you cannot prevent a major catastrophe, but you can build an organization that is battle-ready, that has high morale, and also has been through a crisis, knows how to behave, trusts itself, and where people trust one another.[1]

If you are alive, you will experience challenges and times of testing. "Everyone who wants to live a godly life in Christ Jesus will be persecuted,"[2] said the apostle Paul, and there is good reason to believe, because of the fact that much of what happens here in the physical realm is an echo of battles being fought in the spiritual,[3] that our ministry will most likely be assaulted by the forces of darkness when it is at its most effective. If you are successful, opposition will be your reward.

Sources of Obstacles

The unexpected success—A ministry prays for blessing (additional opportunities and resources to meet needs), but when the floodgates of heaven are opened and God answers their prayer the new opportunities or resources create unforeseen difficulties.

The unexpected failure—an idea that simply doesn't work in meeting needs.

Personal opposition—rendered by spouses or other family members, colleagues or team members in ministry, fellow members at church, members of the community, or those in positions of authority.

The twist of "fate"—someone slips on a banana peel on the sidewalk in front of your ministry office and sues you for $5 million.

Management mistakes—poor leadership practices that get you in hot water with your team members, those who give permissions, the observing public, or perhaps worst of all, the members of your target group.

Character issues—the effects of personal struggles with temptation and sin. More than one ministry leader has come crashing down like a fiery meteorite following seemingly overnight revelations of sexual misconduct or other sinful behavior.

Complacency and torpidity—very few ministries can survive some of the more detrimental effects of long-term institutionalization. The landscape of our nation's educational system is littered with colleges that were once dynamic seminaries or Christian training schools, but yielded in time to the subversively slow process of complacency and compromise.

As we examine the Scriptures, we discover that obstacles are either external, internal, or unseen.

> *External obstacles*—opposition from others, circumstances, hardships
> *Internal obstacles*—character flaws, temptation, sin, impatience
> *Unseen obstacles*—Satan's efforts to oppose God's plan in our lives

It is interesting to note that external obstacles are almost always more easily overcome than are internal obstacles.

How God Uses Obstacles

The story of Job demonstrates that the obstacles we confront are allowed by the Lord to accomplish his purpose in our lives. As we consider how he does this we can identify four distinct purposes for obstacles:

- To develop our personal character
- To redirect us to a greater purpose
- To revise our plans and implement God's perfect timing
- To bring glory to God as he helps us to overcome them

No matter what the purpose for an obstacle in our life is, our attitude toward it is to be the same. That attitude is embodied by Romans 8:28, "And we know that in all things God works for the good of those who love him, who have been called according to his purpose."

Obstacles as Character Development

Maintaining God's Perspective

As a young man Joseph, the son of Jacob, was one man who got all the bad breaks. From our perspective, he had every right to be bitter toward God. Instead, his attitude was exemplary. He maintained perspective and strove to serve God where he was, in every situation. He realized that all things he experienced came from the hand of God, and had a divine purpose: "You intended to harm me, but God intended it for good to accomplish what is now being done, the saving of many lives" (Gen. 50:20).

Joseph was falsely accused despite serving faithfully and spent years in a terrible dungeon where he faced bitter disappointments before finally rising to authority by the grace of God in a foreign land. The end results of his trials were glorious. He literally was placed in a position to save the lives of his family and the future of his nation. But these results didn't come without a price—years of indescribable suffering.

Confronting obstacles frequently means dealing with discouragement. If anyone had reason for discouragement, it was Joseph. No doubt he must have struggled with discouragement at times, although there is no record of this struggle. But how would he have dealt with discouragement?

The overriding tone of Joseph's life can be summed up as: He was a man of focused faith in God's ability to deliver. This otherworldliness characterized his life as a child, and it carried him through the many difficult years. He trusted God to finish what he had begun, and endured with longsuffering the trials that took place in the meantime. Like Joseph, we must set our minds on the things that are above, and endure obstacles faithfully and patiently!

Taking a Deeper Cut

It was obvious to those who observed the young man Moses that the hand of God was on his life for a special purpose. He had been miraculously saved from being killed, and was raised in the court of Pharaoh with a royal education.

Yet Moses' first attempt at intervening on behalf of God's people ended in chaos. When he saw a Hebrew slave being abused, he stepped in and killed the oppressor. His premature actions led to his exile from Egypt.

But God had a purpose for Moses' forty-year reeducation as a shepherd in the desert. During that time, he gained intimate knowledge of the desert and how to survive in it. But more importantly, in the desert Moses grew in the knowledge of the Lord, and God molded his character through this experience, building into the impulsive young hotshot humility and patience.

Do we value God's development of our character? If so, we will use discouragement and failures as the mortar and bricks that God uses to conform us more into the image of his Son.

Overcoming Discouragements

Often we aren't prepared for the fact that our greatest discouragements can come on the heels of our most exciting ministry successes.

God used Elijah to prophesy his judgment on Ahab, that wicked king of Israel, and his even more thoroughly wicked wife, Jezebel. Leadership for Elijah was definitely a foul weather job. After prophesying three years of drought, he had to go into hiding while the king and queen killed godly prophets and scoured the land for him as well.

But after three years it was time for a showdown, the so-called shoot-out at the Carmel corral. Elijah called the false prophets on the carpet. God sent fire from heaven to devour the sacrifice on the Lord's altar, and then the 450 fleeing, false prophets were slaughtered. Then Elijah prayed, and where there had been cloudless skies a downpour came, ending the three years of drought. Running in the power of the Spirit, Elijah even beat the king's chariot in a footrace. For the man of God, it was a very good day. Elijah must have been heady with success.

Burnout, however, is one of the greatest challenges confronting Christians who are involved in ministry. Because we harbor the notion that burnout comes only as a result of ministry failures, we often are caught flatfooted when burnout follows on the heels of our greatest ministry successes. It took only a few dark words by Jezebel to completely change Elijah's mood. Rather than shrug off her empty threats and send her to join her false prophets, Elijah found himself discouraged and once again in hiding—this time self-imposed hiding.

Elijah made a forty-day journey all the way to Horeb, the mountain of God, where he could hide and nurse his wounds. It was there that the Lord began to minister to him: "What are you doing here, Elijah?"

Elijah laid out his complaints. He had been good and faithful, doing everything God had asked, but he was the only prophet left, and now "they" were trying to kill him!

The Lord's response was full of tenderness. He told Elijah to come out and witness the passage of the Lord. There was a mighty wind—but the Lord wasn't in it. Then, an earthquake—but God wasn't in the earthquake. Next, a fire—but God wasn't in the fire either. Finally, Elijah heard a gentle voice speaking, as in a whisper to his soul. He knew. That was the Lord.

That gentle whisper told Elijah the truth. He was not the only one left; God had reserved seven thousand others in Israel who had not kissed the lips of Baal. God's point was gentle, but it was very, very clear: You're not alone. There are always others whom God will use to do his will if we cannot or will not.

The fact is, *God does not need us.* Who are *we,* anyway? The entire world does *not* depend on our resources. Jesus said, "Take my yoke upon you and learn from me, for I am gentle and humble in heart, and you will find rest for your souls. For my yoke is easy and my burden is light" (Matt. 11:29–30).

If God chooses to use you to accomplish his will and to minister to others, that is not a burden; it is a blessing! Christ promised we would be rewarded for our work, but he has not recruited us because he needs our help.

Counteracting Burnout

Moses was another biblical leader who faced burnout. Moses sat day and night, mediating the disputes for, and counseling literally millions of Israelites. Moses' father-in-law Jethro saw that Moses was in danger: "What you are doing is not good," he said. "You and these people who come to you will only wear yourselves out. The work is too heavy for you; you cannot handle it alone" (Exod. 18:17–18). Thus, Jethro suggested a structure for training key leaders and delegating to them the tasks that Moses had taken on himself. Moses knew good advice when he saw it, so he implemented the structure and found timely relief.

Frequently burnout comes when we think or act as if we alone can do the work of ministry that God is calling our team to. Careful and consistent training of team members, along with disciplined delegation, will prove to be an effective guard against burnout.

Jethro's words to Moses also underscore the need for a support group that can undergird us in prayer, suggest ways that we can be more effective, and give encouragement when we are discouraged.

It is encouraging that God did not harshly rebuke Elijah for his discouragement. Instead he whispered, and ministered to him. He reassured and calmed. And then he simply said, in essence, "Okay, get back to work now" (1 Kings 19:15–18).

The fact is, we're human beings. We tire easily, we run for a while on vapors, and then we come quickly to the end of our own resources. He knows we need rest and renewal, and that is why Christ said, "The Sabbath was made for man, not man for the Sabbath" (Mark 2:27). And sometimes, once one is rested, it is simply a matter of gritting your teeth, rolling up your sleeves, and jumping right back into the battle.

Today, Christian leaders are experiencing burnout at an unprecedented rate. As a society, our pace is more hectic, our information overload more dizzying, our environmental challenges more complex and stimulating than has been experienced by any society at any time in history. Couple this with a high-stress culture that devalues long-term commitments and such character attributes as tenacity and patience, and the danger of burning out is greater than ever before. We must renew our commitment to developing the character and the skills that will enable us to avoid this ministry-killing malady.

Making Mid-Course Corrections

Sometimes obstacles come because God wants to redirect our efforts in order that his greater purpose may be accomplished.

On one of Paul's missionary journeys, he was headed into the province of Asia, fully intending to preach the gospel there and plant churches in the same way he had been doing. But an interesting thing happened at the border of Mysia: "They tried to enter Bithynia, but the Spirit of Jesus would not allow them to. So they passed by Mysia and went down to Troas" (Acts 16:7–8). That night Paul had a vision of a man of Macedonia, standing and begging him, "Come over to Macedonia and help us" (v. 9). "After Paul had seen the vision, we got ready at once to leave for Macedonia, concluding that God had called us to preach the gospel to them" (v. 10).

Unlike Balaam, Paul's strategic plan wasn't so rigidly structured that he failed to recognize when God was putting obstacles in his path in order to change his direction. He maintained flexibility and listened to the Lord for new directions.

We all know of ministries that have set themselves on an inflexible course, and then have been unwilling to change when the circumstances and opportunities demanded it. Invariably, these ministries lose relevance and slowly die. God's will is often manifested through an open door as well as through a closed door. We must follow him closely and carefully in order to be able to tell the one from the other.

Waiting for God's Timing

Sometimes a particular ministry project or method is the right thing to do, but it is the wrong time. God raised Moses to be the deliverer of his people; but he intended that this delivery take place in a certain way after Moses had spent his forty years as a shepherd. When Moses sought by his own strength to deliver an oppressed Hebrew slave, disaster resulted.

King David provides another interesting example. David's deepest desire was to build for the Lord a permanent dwelling place, a magnificent temple. But it was not to be; the timing was not yet perfect. David's life had been one of conflicts and battles, and God desired that his temple be constructed in the context of an Israel at peace with its neighbors. God used David to prepare the way for the temple, but it wasn't until David had passed on that his son, Solomon, was released to actually begin the building.

Just because we have a passion for ministry does not guarantee that we will ever see our goal realized. Jim Elliot never saw the fruit of his labors among the Auca Indians, and it wasn't until after he and his colleagues shed their own blood that the door for ministry was opened and God began to revive the tribe. Moses himself never entered the Promised Land, but the work of his life resulted in Joshua's leading the children of Israel there. David never saw the temple, but his work made it possible for Israel to build it after he had passed on. Our faithfulness in ministry is required by God whether or not we ever actually see its fruit in our day. But we have comfort in the fact that ". . . he who began a good work in you will carry it on to completion until the day of Christ Jesus" (Phil. 1:6).

Dealing with Opposition

Nehemiah was a Jew exiled to Persia during the fourth century B.C. Nehemiah was an overcomer by nature, having attained the influential position of cupbearer to King Artaxerxes and also having attained the king's trust in his faithfulness and integrity. The result was that he requested, and was subsequently appointed by the king, to be governor of Judea.

Nehemiah had heard reports of a Jerusalem in disgrace, which were confirmed by a personal trip. He was a man of passion, who "sat down and wept" after he saw the need, and didn't rise from his supplication and mourning for many days. Having seen the serious need with his own eyes, Nehemiah then took on the challenging task of rousing his fellow Israelites to his personal vision of restoring the wall and the good name of Jerusalem in an exceedingly hostile political climate.

Nehemiah's obstacles to fulfilling his dream were legion. First he had to secure the permission of those in authority to grant safe passage and provide resources for the rebuilding. This would be no small feat, and he knew it; it was accomplished through much prayer and fasting. Second, he had to transmit his vision to disenfranchised Hebrews, and lead them in a difficult rebuilding project fraught with challenges. This was accomplished by Nehemiah's expert use of his position and authority to inspire, to give ownership of the mission, to delegate, and to oversee the tasks.

Serious opposition arose during the course of this project. Neighboring political officials perceived Nehemiah's efforts to be a threat to their security and high positions, and they began to oppose him. They first employed ridicule; then when this didn't work, they planned violence. When the violence was thwarted, they engaged in further psychological warfare, sending in decoys with words of discouragement for Nehemiah. They literally engaged in everything they could think of to stop his vision.

The threat was so serious that Nehemiah's team members, at one point, had to work with a sword in one hand and a trowel in the other! Keeping one step ahead of the opposition took much of Nehemiah's time and energy. But in spite of this, the wall builders prevailed, and the wall was restored in an amazing fifty-two days.

However, the story doesn't end there. In spite of the great victory celebration after the task was completed, Nehemiah still had to deal with severe internal conflicts. Religious leaders neglected their tasks and compromised their principles. Some were exacting usury and bleeding the economy dry. But Nehemiah boldly confronted each obstacle, responding quickly and surely. He demonstrated his abilities as one of the most skillful project leaders recorded in the pages of Scripture.

Did Nehemiah experience discouragement in all this? Several times it seems that discouragement was unavoidable. Once, after discovering the destructive usurious practices of countrymen, the prophet admits that he "was angry"—probably an understatement.

But each time Nehemiah encountered a potential discouragement, he turned in prayer to the Lord. He poured out his fears and his objections to God, and let the results rest in his hands:

> Hear us, O our God, for we are despised. Turn their insults back on their own heads. Give them over as plunder in a land of captivity.
>
> *Nehemiah 4:4*

> They were all trying to frighten us, thinking, "Their hands will get too weak for the work, and it will not be completed." But I prayed, "Now strengthen my hands."
>
> *Nehemiah 6:9*

Nehemiah exemplified the saying: "Pray like it all depends on God—and work like it all depends on you."

Strategies Nehemiah used in leading his team to complete the task included:

Understand the enemy. Nehemiah listened carefully and sought to be kept aware of the plots of the enemy. He worked proactively to foil his opponent's plans before they could do him damage. He recognized the tactic of the enemy to use misinformation in an attempt to dissuade him from his goal. These are the same tactics that Satan will use to try to stop Christians today. First Peter 5:8 says, "Be self-controlled and alert. Your enemy the devil prowls around like a roaring lion looking for someone to devour." The Greek word-picture is of an old, toothless lion who hasn't much true power to destroy but who can certainly frighten his victims with his loud roaring. Nehemiah knew how to respond to this type of tactic—he remained self-controlled and alert.

Bold and immediate confrontation of problems. Nehemiah knew that he couldn't sweep a crisis under the rug. Denial is a powerful but destructive human behavior that can cause us, out of fear, to ignore a problem until it is too late to deal with it. Nehemiah dealt with issues promptly and with finality.

Unity. Nehemiah 4:20 shows that he understood the power of unity. His workers established a mutual-aid agreement. If any man was attacked at any point along the wall, a trumpet would be blown and the others would rush to support him. They knew that they had to stand together or die alone.

Spiritual discernment. At one point a colleague attempted to discourage Nehemiah and get him to hide by giving false reports of a threat to his life. Nehemiah prayed and saw through the ruse, recognizing that his enemies had hired the colleague to oppose him.

More and more in these last days, we will face opposition from others whose way of life is threatened by our service. When John Perkins established Harambee Center in an urban neighborhood in Pasadena, California, drug lords in the neighborhood perceived his ministry as a direct threat to their livelihood. He received death threats and his neighborhood center was firebombed four separate times. Yet John knew that God desired to do a work of ministry through Harambee Center, and he persisted in prayer and courageous faithfulness in spite of the threats and the violence. Today, the drug lords have moved away, and Harambee Center stands as a testimony to the Lord's grace and the perseverance of the Perkins family.

Confronting Spiritual Obstacles

Some obstacles come as the result of a direct spiritual attack by satanic forces against God's plan for our lives and ministries. Paul informed the Thessalonian believers of one such attack as he wrote his first epistle to them.

> But, brothers, when we were torn away from you a short time (in person, not in thought), out of our intense longing we made every effort to see you. For we wanted to come to you—certainly I, Paul, did, again and again—but Satan stopped us.
>
> *1 Thessalonians 2:17–18*

Paul recognized the handiwork of the evil one in preventing the ministry that he desired to do. Throughout the New Testament we see Satan intervening in ministry. Paul also attributed to a "messenger of Satan" his "thorn in the flesh" (2 Cor. 12:7–9) sent to torment him.

Paul's response to any incursion of Satan in his ministry was to get down on his knees and begin doing some serious spiritual warfare. "Three times I pleaded with the Lord to take it away from me," he wrote of the affliction from his unseen oppressor (2 Cor. 12:8). But the Lord's response was, "My grace is sufficient for you, for my power is made perfect in weakness" (2 Cor. 12:9). Just as God in his wisdom allowed Satan to test Job, so he allowed the messenger of Satan to remain in Paul's life!

As we go to prayer to discern and do spiritual warfare against unseen enemies, our first responsibility is to listen to God. If God continues to allow the evil one to oppress us, what is his purpose in doing so? What attitude does the mind of Christ desire us to assume toward our torment?

Satan prevented Paul from visiting the Thessalonians, but the apostle realized that God had a more perfect plan. He sent Timothy to strengthen and encourage the church in Thessalonica. Timothy brought back good news about the steadfast faith of the Thessalonians, which Paul says was a great encouragement to him in the midst of his trials. So, although Satan sought to disrupt—and indeed, succeeded in disrupting—Paul's heartfelt plans, God had a more perfect way in mind.

Few Christians devote much concern to Satan's strategy for tripping them up. Yet Scripture is clear on this point: Satan is a schemer who spends his time brainstorming ways to outwit us and foil our plans. Paul acknowledged this in 2 Corinthians 2:10–11 when he said, "I have forgiven in the sight of Christ for your sake, in order that Satan might not outwit us. For we are not unaware of his schemes."

It probably is no great stretch to postulate that our puny mortal brains are severely outclassed when it comes to engaging in mental contests with Lucifer, the most magnificent among God's created beings. Fortunately, as God's children we have the mind of Christ (1 Cor. 2:16). We can ask for the godly wisdom that we lack (James 1:5). The weapons we fight with are not the weapons of the world.

> On the contrary, they have divine power to demolish strongholds. We demolish arguments and every pretension that sets itself up against the knowledge of God, and we take captive every thought to make it obedient to Christ.
>
> *2 Corinthians 10:4–5*

There's not much to relish about the prospect of being "tormented" by unseen spiritual forces. But sooner or later, it happens to every believer who desires to do effective and compassionate ministry in the name of Christ. Fortunately, we can take encouragement in the knowledge that God has promised us

- divine awareness of the devil's scheming
- the power of prayer
- the comfort of knowing that his strength is made perfect in weakness—that God's best always comes after Satan does his worst

You're in Good Company

If our ministry is to be effective, each of us will encounter obstacles, internal and external, seen and unseen. God uses these obstacles to strengthen our character, redirect us, exercise his perfect timing, and glorify himself. He also promises ultimate victory over our trials!

> You, dear children, are from God and have overcome them, because the one who is in you is greater than the one who is in the world.
>
> *1 John 4:4*

It is a privilege and a blessing to suffer for the name of Christ. We are then in good company with the Suffering Servant himself, who was "despised and rejected by men, a man of sorrows, and familiar with suffering" (Isaiah 53:3).

Consider the crisis not something to be feared and avoided, but a time of testing to be anticipated, well prepared for, and embraced.

> Whenever and however the crisis comes, it is a true time of judgment, a God-given opening to be seized with courage, entered in faith, and pursued with passion.[4]

Action Idea Checklist

- ☐ Ask the Lord to develop godly character that grows stronger in the midst of adversity and challenges.
- ☐ Deepen your personal devotional life.
- ☐ Maintain physical health through diet, rest, and exercise.
- ☐ Renew spiritual and emotional reserves through Sabbath times.
- ☐ Cultivate spouse and family relationships.
- ☐ Establish an intercession team; communicate at least monthly.
- ☐ Build personal friendships and support systems.
- ☐ Set aside regular times for reflection and refocusing, both personally and in a team setting.
- ☐ Develop a team of intercessors to help you fight the spiritual battles.

Add your own follow-up items on the next page.

Conclusion: Mission and Ministry

Ministry through the Lens of Christ's Commands

Maria is a widowed believer in an impoverished section of Mexico, not unlike the woman in Christ's parable of the widow's mite. Like so many others, she found herself caught in the grip of homelessness and despair. But Maria turned her cry heavenward, asking the Lord to provide her miraculously with a simple home as a testimony of his faithfulness. "I will open it up to others, and use it to tell them about you!" she promised.

One day Maria met Jim and John Jubile who were working on a construction project in the area. As the Jubiles got to know Maria, they learned of her need and of her desire to use a home to share the gospel. They felt moved of the Lord to build Maria a simple home.

Maria knew that the Lord had miraculously provided an answer to her prayers through the Jubile brothers. Like the former demoniac of the Gerasenes, Maria began joyfully inviting friends, neighbors, and street people into her home to share what the Lord had done for her. Many lives were touched for Christ as a result of these two young brothers' act of compassion. Without sharing a tract or preaching a sermon, their simple act of mercy fulfilled the Great Commission in one small but needy corner of the world.

A Unified Purpose

What is our purpose as Christians? What is the purpose of the church?

The Westminster Catechism broadly defines our purpose as Christians as "to glorify God." But Scripture, in two places, gets more specific on how we mortals can accomplish that glorification. We call these specifics the Great Commandment and the Great Commission.

The Great Commandment

"Love the Lord your God with all your heart and with all your soul and with all your mind." This is the first and greatest commandment. And the second is like it: "Love your neighbor as yourself." All the Law and the Prophets hang on these two commandments.

Matthew 22:37–40

The Great Commission

Therefore go and make disciples of all nations, baptizing them in the name of the Father and of the Son and of the Holy Spirit, and teaching them to obey everything I have commanded you. And surely I am with you always, to the very end of the age.

Matthew 28:19–20

What is the relationship between the Great Commandment and the Great Commission? What is our responsibility toward these instructions of Christ?

We have traditionally compartmentalized our ministry mind-set along these two lines, assigning foreign missions as well as personal evangelism to the Great Commission, and what is traditionally called "compassion ministry" (feeding the hungry and meeting other human needs), as well perhaps as "one-another" ministry, to the Great Commandment. But are these divisions artificial? Is there some sort of synthesis between the Great Commandment and the Great Commission, our compassionate need-meeting work and our evangelistic work, that would help us to think more clearly about our mission on this planet?

Throughout this book we have offered examples of ministries that seek to fulfill, in the same stroke, both the Great Commandment and the Great Commission. Steve Sjogren's ministry is a good example. When Steve, the pastor of Vineyard Christian Fellowship in Ohio, first began planting the church, he had a vision for one thousand people. But at his first meeting, in spite of months of hard work, only thirty-five attended. Frustrated and discouraged, he heard the Lord speak directly to his heart: *If you will befriend my friends then you'll have more people than you know what to do with.*

But how to do that? Steve started his search for answers by looking in the Scriptures. "I began to look . . . for the kinds of people Jesus spent his short ministry interacting with. I began to see something new. Although Jesus loved everyone, he apparently enjoyed spending the better part of his time with three types of people: the *poor,* the *sick,* and the *lost.* Even the apostles came from the hurting of society."

Steve relates how he then went to the local mall to "people watch." He recalls, "As I looked into the faces of person after person, I realized almost everyone is experiencing a significant level of misery. Jesus desires to touch and heal their pain. Somehow my job was to be around and minister to those people. But how?"

An idea began to form, which he articulated as: "If we could somehow lighten some of the pain these people are going through—even for a moment—maybe we could get their attention. By *serving our way into their hearts,* maybe we could gain their ears."

Steve simply watched people, asking himself what they needed that the church could help provide. One of the simple things he saw was dirty cars. He organized a car-washing crew, which had by the end of their first afternoon ministered to forty people. Long, cold winter months in Cincinnati leave accumulated road salt on cars, causing serious corrosion. Car washing there is a significant act of service. "Amazingly," Steve says, "many wouldn't believe we would do something for free—no strings attached." Naturally the beneficiaries of the car washing inquired as to why, so Steve had a couple of "designated evangelists," who shared who they were and that they were simply doing it "just because God loves you."

Since that first car wash, Vineyard has sponsored more than one hundred other similar outreach projects. The church has grown from thirty-five to over 2,800 in eight years and planted more than ten churches. Many people, says Steve, are attracted to a church that demonstrates that it is in touch with its community.

Steve views the relationship between the Great Commandment and the Great Commission like the relationship between planting and watering the crops, and the harvest. Both activities—planting-watering and harvesting—are part of the same goal, reaping the benefits of the crops. Our goal must be to obey Christ and to reconcile men to God (2 Cor. 5:20); fulfilling both the Great Commandment and the Great Commission are integral parts to this.

Too often, says Steve, Christians have sought to fulfill the Great Commission through philosophical or theological means. But the defenses that people erect to the gospel are defenses erected at these levels. Steve tells of one successful businessman who was brought to tears by those who washed his car and then shared the gospel with him:

> I believe he was touched because we went around all of his established defenses that had kept people—and God—away from his life . . . in a sense, we broke the rules and were not "fighting fair." We sneaked in the back door of his life where he was least expecting it—his heart—and made a significant impact.
>
> By coming to pre-Christians with a desire to serve them and relieve their pain we avoid battling in a mental or verbal arena and go right to their hearts. I haven't seen much fruit in trying to convert people at a head-to-head level—apologetics, telling, arguing—but a heart-to-heart witness is hard to resist. As we go for the hearts of people we bypass their defenses.[1]

As Steve points out, Romans 2:4 demonstrates that God is our model for a synthesis of the Great Commandment and the Great Commission: It is the kindness of God that leads to repentance.

Pastor Ray Bakke, author of *The Urban Christian,* notes that the urban poor have less of a problem synthesizing Great Commandment social action with Great Commission evangelism.

> It is only in our rich Western countries that we have the luxury of dividing two sides of [this] common coin. John Stott uses such images as the two belonging together like two blades of a pair of scissors or two wings of a bird. Christians who are still debating these priorities often miss the point that social action is not done in order to communicate the gospel but as

a sign or evidence that the gospel has already been received and acted upon. Social ministry is the loving service of Christians set free by the risen Lord from sins and bondage.[2]

Bob Stratton is pastor of Church on the Street, one of the most unusual churches you will ever find, a church without walls that meets each Sunday afternoon in a vacant lot in downtown Los Angeles. The vision for the church began with his father, Robert. Bob recalls, "We went down there with grocery bags full of sandwiches, in teams, and that evolved into one-on-one ministry, which evolved into this church on the street. The Holy Spirit was poured out and we saw tremendous miracles, people who were healed and delivered. Shattered lives were restored through acts of kindness and love."

When people band together, things get accomplished. Large churches can be less effective than small churches if that small church is full of people who are committed to accomplishing a work together.

God works when people go out to minister real deeds of mercy to others. Out of that mission multitudes of people will get saved and delivered. These are acts of evangelism; the world is won to Jesus Christ because of his good acts. That's not *why* we're saved, but that's *how* people come into his kingdom.

Rev. Phil Starr is the director of Outreach Ministries at Church on the Way, a church known for its exquisite philosophy and practice of *worship.* Phil sees *worship of God* as the thread that links outreach ministry to evangelism.

"Our people reach out in the community, out of their understanding of the power of worship. They reach out in love, wherever their calling takes them, teaching worship and bringing an awareness of Christ as the one who can make the difference in people's lives—whether those people are in the suburbs, or on skid row, or death row.

"The Pacoima park ministry [one of the church's first ministries] always began with worship. Before they opened the gates to let people in, the workers came before the Lord in worship, and moved into spiritual warfare so that God would give them not only a prophetic understanding of what he wanted to do, but also that they would be sensitive to each person's needs as they came through the line—not evangelizing them, not preaching to them, just being there to ask, 'Can we pray for you?' If they had a need, we ministered to that need and sent them on their way to the clothing selection area. Doing this, eighteen hundred people in the last three and a half years of ministry came to know the Lord—without one evangelistic sermon being preached."

George Caywood, director of Los Angeles' Union Rescue Mission, once addressed a group of seminary students at Campus Crusade for Christ's International School of Theology, located on the outskirts of San Bernardino, California. "Suppose the Christians in San Bernardino," he told them, "repented of materialism. Let's say they went into the community and saw to it that there were no widows with unpainted houses, no one sleeping in the streets, and no hungry children in the whole city of San Bernardino." (Since there are more than one hundred churches in the city, this would not be an impossible proposition.) "After their hard work, suppose you people took your *Four Spiritual Laws* door-to-door. What difference would it make?"

George recalls, "The whole crowd of theology students seemed to throw themselves back in their chairs and look off in the distance, with a powerful longing for something as wonderful as that to be true." His point was that consistent and thorough obedience to the Great Commandment would make a huge difference to the manageability of our task in obeying the Great Commission. His conclusion:

> Because of the failure of Christians to act out what is clearly taught in the gospel, our evangelists face the difficulty of trying to win an essentially dark and unsalted society. Evangelists have to resort to techniques with which they aren't comfortable, such as taking surveys. If the world was salted and enlightened by the behavior of Christians the lost could be won effectively.[3]

When God commanded Moses regarding the manufacture of the tabernacle, he gave very explicit instructions for the materials to be used. Many of the items used inside the sanctuary, for example, the ark of the covenant, the posts and table on which it rested, and the poles that carried the table, were constructed of acacia, or *shittah* wood overlaid with pure gold.

The *shittim,* or acacia trees, were thorny and very hardy and grew where no others would. (In Southern California the equivalent would be mesquite.) They would be plentiful in desert areas, but difficult to work, and therefore probably more expensive than a wood like pine.

Why did God go to the trouble of specifying a difficult and expensive wood if it was simply going to be covered up with gold? Obviously, from the outside, all you would see would be the gold. We would be duly impressed with that, and probably wouldn't know or care if the inside was acacia, or some other more reasonably priced (and easily worked) material.

The relationship between our good works and evangelism is something like the relationship between those two materials that comprised the furniture of God. Evangelism, which can be likened to the gold, must be laid over a difficult and expensive foundation—good works. Too often, in our impatience for quick results, we try to put the gold on a foundation of pine, or on no foundation at all. We like to see big stadiums full of people thronging to accept Christ. But are we willing to put down in the city the slow and tedious foundation of good works that must precede that precious harvest?

Traditionally, evangelism has been thought to be an event in which you aggressively invaded the privacy of strangers in order to present cognitive arguments for salvation. Your skills as a soul winner were affirmed when these victims fell to their knees and repented of their sins. If you weren't willing to stuff down your terror and walk up to a complete stranger in the mall, bearing your Bible before you as a weapon, then there was obviously something wrong with your faith. Of course, if they rejected you, you could be comforted by the fact that these hell-bound sinners weren't really rejecting *you;* they were rejecting God.

Larry Short attended a Christian college in which students were required to participate periodically in this sort of so-called evangelism:

> Every time I went out I suffered from an enormous load of doubt, the feeling that there was some important *missing element* to what we were doing; but then, every once in awhile it would work and someone would pray with me to receive Christ. So the obvious conclusion was that my doubts were the result of my own weak faith.

Many years later I joined Community Baptist Church, a church of a different stripe. One of my first tasks was to take a membership orientation class in which there was some training about personal evangelism. Due to my earlier experience, I approached this with due fear.

This time, however, there was a different focus, which had the effect of freeing me from my previous anxieties. Effective personal evangelism, or lifestyle evangelism as I was told it was called, was more a *process* than an *event,* and one that was based in personal relationships. Dr. Rob Acker modeled for us this sort of evangelism in the relationships he was constantly developing with friends, neighbors, and the unchurched in our community. He got to know people and involved himself in the things they were interested in. He sought to serve them, and won their confidence (and their curiosity!) long before he ever told them, "Jesus loves you and has a wonderful plan for your life." He knew the value of *planting* and *watering* before *harvesting.*

One of the things that CBC does for its members is that it encourages them to discover their spiritual gifts, and then encourages them to figure out how to apply these gifts in ministry. In my case, I found joy in working to save the lives of unborn children from abortion, and in helping to steer their moms clear of its heartache; or in some cases in helping women who had experienced abortions to begin their healing process.

While doing this type of ministry, I began to discover that the Lord was bringing to me clear opportunities for evangelism. Now, I wasn't in this ministry as an evangelist; I had despaired of that long ago. I was in this ministry to save babies and their moms from the exploitation of abortion. But, all of a sudden, here I was acting as an evangelist—and loving every moment of it.

I think back about all the soul-winning methods I studied as a youth, and I wonder why I was so blind to the best method of all—serving people and trying to meet their needs.

True ministry, selfless service to others, stands on its own merit. As Ray Bakke has said, as we seek to obey the Great Commandment of God (we do not do the Great Commandment for the express purpose of fulfilling the Great Commission), we do it out of love and obedience to Christ. The amazing thing is, however, that this obedience simultaneously and inseparably ties part and parcel into the Great

Commission as the *manner* by which we are to reach the world with the gospel, making disciples of all people.

An All-Encompassing Vision

For too long the church has had too narrow of a vision. For too long we've acted like our job is simply to go out and tell people to get saved. Or else, we've acted like our job is simply to be a religious social-service agency where people get their physical needs met. But these are two sides of the same coin, and we aren't given the choice to do one or the other.

Our dual mandate is to *love our neighbors* and to *make disciples of our neighbors,* until we have loved and discipled all people groups. Both can only be truly effective if they are done together; if we employ one without the other, we waste our time with half-measures and end up in a worse position than we were in when we started the job.

Let's broaden our vision! Let's lift up our eyes and sweep them across the fields of this world white with harvest. Let's behold at once the human needs that are waiting to be met, and our compassionate Lord who challenges us to go forth, to the best of our ability, in his name and power, to meet those needs, until he comes again.

Action Idea Checklist

- ☐ Ask God to develop and reproduce ministries integrating the Great Commandment and the Great Commission.
- ☐ Develop a personal plan for evangelizing your network.
- ☐ Evaluate how your compassion ministry results in more and better disciples; take actions to link people to the church.
- ☐ Provide training in relational evangelism; help people design personalized action plans.
- ☐ Plan for ministry improvement, expansion, and reproduction.
- ☐ Ask God to help you, your church, or organization launch new compassion ministries.

Add your own follow-up items on the next page.

Appendix A

*M*eeting Needs in Your Community

Human Needs	Possible Solutions
Aging	Alzheimer's support groups Car repair, home fix-up, yardwork Convalescent home ministry Health care ministries In-home meals and other assistance

Compulsive behaviors	Recovery groups for addictions to:
	    Alcohol and drugs (illegal/prescription)
	    Eating disorders (anorexia, bulimia,
	        compulsive overeating/obesity)
	    Gambling addictions
	    Religious addictions ("toxic faith")
	    Sexual addictions/pornography
	    Workaholism
	Codependency or victims' support groups
	    Children/grandchildren
	    Friends
	    Parents
	    Spouse

Crisis pregnancy	Counseling/pregnancy testing Education Hotlines Post-abortion support groups Sidewalk counseling/intercession Unwed mother's support Victim's advocacy
Disabilities	Advocacy Church building accessibility In-home help for the disabled Support groups for disabled and their loved ones

Loss/grief	Support groups for those suffering from
	    Loss of a loved one
	    Stillborn infant/miscarriage
	    Suicide or murder of a loved one
	Support groups for those responsible
	    for the death of another

Health Problems	AIDS/ARC/HIV outreach ministries
	Environmental illness support
	Hospice ministry
	Medical/dental clinics
	Mental health counseling
	Support for those in chronic pain
	Support for those with chronic illness or disease
	Support for victims and families of the terminally ill
Marital/family problems	Support for abused spouses
	Counseling for abusers
	Adoption services
	Barrenness support
	Blended families support groups
	Divorce counseling/support
	Marital counseling
	Money management support
	Support for victims and perpetrators of infidelity
	Support for parents of homosexual children
	Support for parents of troubled children
Poverty	Advocacy
	Homeless outreach/shelters
	Hunger and development ministries
	Loss-of-job support groups
	Orphans/widows support
	Vocational training
Prisoners	Helps for families of prisoners
	Pen pal ministries
	Rehabilitation/training ministries
	Visitation
Victims	Support groups for victims of
	Abortion
	Cults/satanic ritual abuse
	Incarcerated parents/children
	Incest
	Natural disasters
	Rape
	Spousal/child abuse
	Uncontrolled emotions (overcoming anger, fear)
	Violent crime

These represent just the tip of the iceberg. Consider the needs in your community, and how you can help reach out to hurting people in the name of Jesus.

Appendix B

A Christian Version of the Twelve Steps

Courtesy of Ed Carey

Step One

"We admitted we were powerless over our addictions and compulsive behaviors—that our lives had become unmanageable."

> Luke 8:22–25
> 2 Corinthians 1:8–11
> Romans 7:18–8:2

Step Two

"We came to believe that a power greater than ourselves could restore us to sanity."

> Matthew 6:28–34
> Matthew 15:27–28
> Psalm 30:1–3

Step Three

"We made a decision to turn our will and our lives over to the care of God."

> John 3:16
> Matthew 11:28–30
> Psalm 32:7–10

Step Four

"We made a searching and fearless moral inventory of ourselves."

> Proverbs 28:13
> Matthew 7:1–5
> Psalm 139:23–24

Step Five

"We admitted to God, to ourselves and to another human being the exact nature of our wrongs."

> James 5:13–16
> Psalm 32:3–5
> 1 John 1:8–10

Step Six

"We were entirely ready to have God remove all these defects of character."

> Romans 6:1–14
> Psalm 51:10–12
> 1 John 1:8–10

Step Seven

"We humbly asked Him to remove our shortcomings."

> Psalm 40:1–3
> Luke 11:9–13
> Luke 18:10–14

Step Eight

"We made a list of all persons we had harmed and became willing to make amends to all of them."

> Matthew 5:23–24

Step Nine

"We made direct amends to such people wherever possible, except when to do so would injure them or others."

> Luke 19:1–9

Step Ten

"We continued to take personal inventory and when we were wrong promptly admitted it."

> Matthew 6:9–15
> 1 John 1:8–10
> James 1:19–22

Step Eleven

"We sought through prayer and meditation to improve our conscious contact with God, praying only for knowledge of His will for us and the power to carry that out."

> Psalm 27
> Psalm 105:1–5
> Psalm 119:1–12

Step Twelve

"Having had a spiritual awakening as a result of these steps, we tried to carry this message to others and to practice these principles in all our affairs."

> John 15:5–15
> 1 Peter 4:1–6
> Titus 2:15–3:8
> 1 Timothy 4:15–16

The Twelve Steps
of Alcoholics Anonymous

1. We admitted we were powerless over alcohol—that our lives had become unmanageable.
2. Came to believe that a Power greater than ourselves could restore us to sanity. 3. Made
a decision to turn our will and our lives over to the care of God *as we understood Him*. 4.
Made a searching and fearless moral inventory of ourselves. 5. Admitted to God, to ourselves
and to another human being the exact nature of our wrongs. 6. Were entirely ready to have
God remove all these defects of character. 7. Humbly asked Him to remove our shortcomings.
8. Made a list of all persons we had harmed, and became willing to make amends to them
all. 9. Made direct amends to such people wherever possible, except when to do so would
injure them or others. 10. Continued to take personal inventory and when we were wrong
promptly admitted it. 11. Sought through prayer and meditation to improve our conscious
contact with God, *as we understood Him*, praying only for knowledge of His will for us and
the power to carry that out. 12. Having had a spiritual awakening as the result of these
steps, we tried to carry this message to alcoholics, and to practice these principles in all
our affairs.

> *The Twelve Steps are reprinted and adapted with permission of Alcoholics Anony-*
> *mous World Services, Inc. Permission to reprint and adapt the Twelve Steps does not*
> *mean that A.A. has reviewed or approved the contents of this publication nor that*
> *A.A. agrees with the views expressed herein. A.A. is a program of recovery from alco-*
> *holism—use of the Twelve Steps in connection with programs and activities which*
> *are patterned after A.A., but which address other problems, does not imply other-*
> *wise.*

Appendix C

Blank Forms

Core Values Chart
  Principles/ Resulting Values

Core Values Chart
  Core Values/Resulting Behaviors

Ministry Flowchart

Core Values Chart for: ————————————————
Principles ————————▶ *Resulting Values*

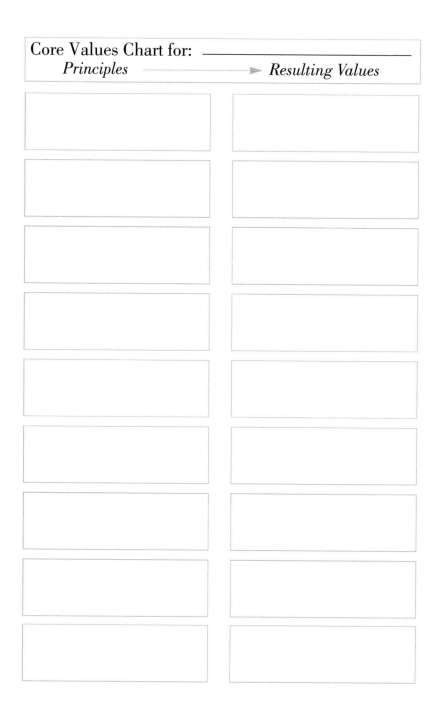

Core Values Chart for: ————————————
Core Values ——————▸ *Resulting Behaviors*

Ministry: —————————

Ministry Flowchart

Target Group/s	Process/Transitions	Program/Goal

Notes

Preface

1. Exodus 23:11, Leviticus 19:10; 23:22, Ruth 2.
2. Acts 4:34–35, 6:1.
3. William G. Travis, "Charles H. Spurgeon and the Poor," *Urban Mission* (September 1992): 29–36.
4. Charles Colson, "Will the Church Miss the Volunteer Revolution?" *Christianity Today* (March 9, 1992): 8.
5. Charles Colson, *Kingdoms in Conflict* (New York: Morrow; Grand Rapids: Zondervan, 1987), 237.
6. Charles Colson, "Will the Church Miss the Volunteer Revolution?", 88.

Chapter 3

1. *JAF Ministries Research Summary* (September 1992), 4.
2. Stephen Covey, *Seven Habits of Highly Effective People* (New York: Simon & Schuster, 1989), 239.
3. Ibid., 240.
4. Ibid., 236.
5. The story of that visit can be found in Robert E. Logan, *Beyond Church Growth*, 67–69.
6. From the foreword to Fred Smith, *Learning to Lead* (Carol Stream, IL: Word Books, 1986), 9–10.
7. Dallas Willard, *The Spirit of Discipline* (San Francisco: Harper & Row, 1988).

Chapter 4

1. Written by Ralph Mattson and Arthur Miller, *Finding a Job You Can Love* (Nashville, TN: Thomas Nelson, 1982).
2. See Carl George and Bob Logan, *Leading and Managing Your Church* (Grand Rapids, MI: Fleming H. Revell, 1987), for more on effective delegation.
3. For more on mentoring, refer to Robert Clinton and Paul Stanley, *Connecting: The Mentoring Relationships You Need to Succeed in Life* (Colorado Springs: NavPress, 1992).

Chapter 5

1. Charles R. Swindoll, *Growing Strong in the Seasons of Life* (Portland, OR: Multnomah Press, 1983), 251.
2. Stephen Covey, *Seven Habits of Highly Effective People*, 35.
3. Peter Drucker, *Managing the Non-Profit Organization* (New York: Harper Collins, 1990), 7–8.
4. Material adapted from Robert E. Logan and Steven L. Ogne, *Church Planter's Toolkit* (Pasadena, CA: Charles E. Fuller Institute of Evangelism and Church Growth, 1991), sections 3 and 4.

Chapter 6

1. Eugene C. Roehlepartain, *The Christian Ministry* (July/August 1992): 7.

2. Quoting Navigators President Jerry White in Christopher B. Adsit, *Personal Disciplemaking* (San Bernardino, CA: Here's Life Publishers, 1988), 17.
3. For more information contact: Overcomers Outreach, 2290 W. Whittier Blvd., Ste. D, La Habra, CA 90631, telephone (310) 697-3994.
4. Adapted from Robert Logan, *Church Planter's Toolkit*, 4–19, 20.

Chapter 7

1. Adapted from Charles Ridley, *How to Select Church Planters* (Pasadena, CA: Fuller Evangelistic Association, 1988).

Chapter 8

1. Peter F. Drucker, *Managing the Nonprofit Organization* (New York: Harper Collins Publishers, 1990), 9.

2 2 Timothy 3:12.
3. Ephesians 6:12.
4. Rowland Croucher, ed., *Still Waters, Deep Waters* (Claremont, CA: Albatross Books, 1987), 163.

Chapter 9

1. Steve Sjogren, "Servant Evangelism: Opening Closed Hearts to God's Love," *Equipping the Saints* (Spring 1992), 18.
2. Ray Bakke, *The Urban Christian* (Downers Grove, IL: InterVarsity Press, 1987), 75.
3. George Caywood, *Escaping Materialism: Living a Life That's Rich Toward God* (Sisters, OR: Questar, 1989), 246.

Index